Welfare in Widecombe
1700-1900

WELFARE IN WIDECOMBE 1700-1900

AN ILLUSTRATED JOURNEY THROUGH LOCAL ARCHIVES

*Best wishes &
enjoy reading
Roger Claxton*

BY

ROGER CLAXTON

PUBLISHED BY WIDECOMBE HISTORY GROUP

Copyright

Printed and published in the United Kingdom

First Printing, 2019

ISBN 978-1-9162849-0-6

Published by:

Widecombe History Group

https://www.widecombe-in-the-moor.com/history

Printed and bound in Great Britain by Short Run Press Ltd.,

Bittern Road, Sowton, Exeter, EX2 7LN.

DEDICATION

This book is dedicated to the poor of Widecombe parish, whose lives must have been a constant struggle, with very little independence of action and constant reliance on others for their survival.

TABLE OF CONTENTS

Table of Contents

LIST OF ILLUSTRATIONS

List of Illustrations

FOREWORD

With ever increasing interest in family heritage and research, this book provides factual information in written form, photographic reproductions and transcripts of original documents, and also many computer links to areas for further reading and research.

Widecombe History Group aims to make the information stored in the various archives containing the history of Widecombe Parish available to the widest possible audience and this book directly furthers this aim.

Roger has, through diligent research and interpretation, brought to light facets of our history written down many years ago. He has made these available for everyone to see and consider, both in the context of their own family history and the wider social provision through the centuries.

Although this book is about "Welfare in Widecombe", the more general information applies to the whole of England from the 11th Century until the end of the period of research in 1900.

"Welfare in Widecombe" contains a great deal of information about how our forefathers dealt with those members of society who were less affluent, less educated, and less healthy than themselves and how attitudes changed and evolved during the two centuries covered in this book.

I hope readers will enjoy the information provided. The subject matter might sometimes be saddening, but it is fully reflective of life in those times. I hope that reading the book will inspire others to go on to further research. This book poses many questions, I hope readers may be inspired to find answers.

Thank you, Roger, for the many hours you have devoted to this book and for the quality of the text and pictures provided.

David Ashman

Chairman, Widecombe History Group

Widecombe-in-the-Moor, October 2019

PREFACE

This work arose out of a large digitisation project to scan and catalogue the Widecombe Parish Chest and other local archive material, including the Widecombe History Group archive. It uses this material as the basis for much of the discussion in the book. A pictorial approach has been taken with almost every referenced document being reproduced and transcribed. The only exceptions to this are where permission could not be obtained to include an image, or the item was only of peripheral interest.

It is a book primarily intended for the general reader rather than for the academic although the latter should also find it of interest as much of the material is newly published.

ACKNOWLEDGEMENTS

Thanks are due to the many volunteers from the Widecombe History Group who have worked diligently on the Widecombe Digital Archive project from its inception in 2011. At the time of writing there are over 17,500 images that have been scanned, catalogued and checked, many of which are online. The project has been organised and run by my wife Ann and without this project the story would have been much more difficult to tell.

I would also like to thank Ann (again) for putting up with me constantly disappearing to write yet another paragraph and also David Ashman for the many hours we spent together photographing and cataloguing images from the archive, having a good old laugh about some of things that we uncovered, and learning a huge amount about pre-1900 Widecombe life.

Thanks are also due to all the people who have kindly granted permission to use images in this work that are in their ownership.

I would also like to thank the staff and volunteers at SW Heritage Trust Devon Archives (https://swheritage.org.uk/devon-archives/) for their help with research and for the images of documents in their care, and similarly the staff and volunteers at Exeter Cathedral Archive (https://www.exeter-cathedral.org.uk/history-heritage/library-archives/) for all their help. Also, thanks are due to Devon Building Control for permission to use the image in Figure 1-3 that shows Widecombe parish in relation to its surrounding parishes, Professor Roger Kain for the image in Figure 1-4 showing the Widecombe parish boundary, and to the Widecombe Parochial Church Council for the numerous images of the select vestry minutes and the charity school accounts (these latter documents are all in the safekeeping of the South West Heritage Trust Devon Archive).

Thanks are also due to Transkribus (website: www.transkribus.eu). Transkribus was used to help with most of the transcriptions in this book. It works by building up a handwriting recognition model (using machine learning techniques) to interpret handwriting based on a hundred or so pages of manually transcribed documents and then using that model to produce transcriptions of further documents automatically. It is then much faster to go through those transcriptions and correct any errors than to do the transcriptions from scratch. Some of the documents were a considerable challenge, but the whole process gained considerably in speed and accuracy as a result of the approach. Also, there is now a 'Widecombe' handwriting recognition model that can be used for further transcriptions should the need arise.

Finally, grateful thanks are due to Tim, David and Ann for carrying out the dedicated, tedious and lengthy task of pointing out my many mistakes and highlighting ways in which improvements could be made. The work is infinitely better as a result of their input.

COVER ILLUSTRATION

The cover illustration is a hand-coloured etching by Thomas Rowlandson (1757-1827) entitled A Select Vestry dating from 1806. It is in the possession of the Metropolitan Museum of Art, New York and is a part of the Elisha Whittelsey Collection donated in 1959. It was donated without restrictions as to re-use, but we are delighted to record our debt to the donors for the ability to use this image. One of the few further known copies of this etching is in the Royal Collection.

SIDNEY AND BEATRICE WEBB

This book includes numerous quotes from Sidney and Beatrice Webb's classic work 'English Local Government: English Poor Law History: Part I. The Old Poor Law' and 'Part II: The Last Hundred Years' published in 1927 and 1929 respectively.

This is worth highlighting here because it is an amazing piece of work, even with its possible flaws and highlights the scholarship and investigative powers of such writing in the days long before the Internet. It is impossible to have anything but admiration for such skills and dedication.

Note on References

The majority of the documents referred to in this book are taken from the Widecombe Digital Archive, an archive of scanned, photographed and catalogued digital material assembled by Widecombe History Group over a number of years and largely available online via: https://widecombearchive.org.uk.

References such as A065, A069 refer to the catalogue numbers given to the individual items in the archive. By going to the above website and entering the references you can bring up details of the documents for viewing. You can also search by name and other criteria. More details on using the archive can be found in Appendix D, and in Appendix E there is help with finding specific items mentioned in the text and in the illustrations.

The more important of the original documents are now deposited at South West Heritage Trust in the Devon Archives Catalogue at Exeter. Their website is:

https://swheritage.org.uk/devon-archives/

Enjoy exploring the archive and investigating the stories hidden within them.

Spelling in Transcripts

Because the vast majority of the documents included here are handwritten, spellings can vary considerably, and mistakes can reasonably be made. Consequently, the spellings shown in the transcripts of those documents have been kept as close to the original as possible.

Also, the use of '*sic*' has been avoided since many spellings vary from today's usage and differing spellings are even used in different pages of the same document. Occasionally words are difficult to identify. They have been left to stand as read.

Making Transcripts Searchable

Transcripts have been provided for almost all of the document images included, even where the document is clearly readable. This is because it enables the transcript to be included in any text search that is carried out using digital versions of this book and makes the content of the document image more accessible.

Preface

ERRORS

There may well be errors in this text. None are known, but factual, transcription and interpretation errors are possible and any that are present are entirely the author's responsibility. Please accept the publishers' apologies for any that you find, and please also send your feedback (see below) so that future editions of the book can be corrected and the errors can be acknowledged in the Additional Resources pages (see below).

LINKS

Links to Internet sites can become out-of-date as sites develop and change. All links are valid as of the date of publication but if a link ceases to work then please accept the author's apologies and try to find the same information through a search engine. The 'Additional Resources' webspace will be used to highlight such problems so it is always worth checking there first.

FEEDBACK

We would love to hear your feedback. Information on errors, further details on the questions that have been posed or the content of the book, especially any new information on any aspect of the poor law or its administration, general comments on the content and anything else in and around the subject matter of the book would be very welcome.

Please send your feedback to: contact@widecombearchive.org.uk.

ADDITIONAL RESOURCES

In order to expand on some of the material in this book and to provide a place for additional information about the topics covered, especially if these arise after publication, and also to incorporate feedback received from readers, a section of the Widecombe Archive website has been reserved to accommodate these resources. This can be found at:

https://widecombearchive.org.uk/welfare

Please visit this resource to see what is available. Please bear in mind that these resources will be added to over time.

REMEMBER TO VISIT:

Additional Resources for this book: widecombearchive.org.uk/welfare

Widecombe Digital Archive: widecombearchive.org.uk

Widecombe Website: widecombe-in-the-moor.com

Widecombe History Group Website: widecombe-in-the-moor.com/history

AND:

For other Widecombe History Group Publications: widecombe-in-the-moor.com/history/publications

CHAPTER 1 INTRODUCTION

FIGURE 1-1: ST PANCRAS CHURCH, WIDECOMBE-IN-THE-MOOR ON A LATE WINTER AFTERNOON IN THE SUN

THE CHURCH HOUSE IS THE BUILDING TO THE LEFT OF THE CHURCH (IMAGE COPYRIGHT THE AUTHOR).

This is a story about welfare provision in Widecombe parish long before the days of our modern welfare state.

There has always been concern for the poor and vulnerable in Britain, even though this might have been influenced at different times by the prevailing politics and norms of the day. This concern has generally been reflected in the laws of the land and it is this law (generally referred to as the Poor Law) that provides the context within which local provision for the less fortunate and vulnerable members of the community can be viewed. There is no doubt that the quality of such provision varied from parish to parish across the country, but certainly in Widecombe it appears to have been relatively well organised and regular in its operation.

This book tells the story of this provision as far as it can be told (in the main) from the records that have been preserved in the Widecombe parish chest and in the Widecombe History Group archive. Many of these records have recently been deposited at the Devon Archives at the South West Heritage Trust and most can be

1

viewed online via the Widecombe Digital Archive website (https://www.widecombearchive.org.uk). Information to help readers use the Widecombe archive is provided below and in Appendix D and Appendix E. This will help the reader whether their aim is to follow-up on items in the text or to research their own ancestors. Some material has also been sourced from the South West Heritage Trust, where it also can be viewed.

Even though there was a statutory basis for welfare provision, which parishes generally followed, nonetheless this provision could vary in quality. In the early days of the Poor Law the external monitoring of the local implementation of these laws was sporadic at best. Also, if, for instance, illness struck, it wasn't easy to drop in to the surgery, especially if you were poor and especially in a moorland parish such as Widecombe. However, it seems that the arm of the law stretched even to Widecombe, and if the poor provision in Widecombe is compared to that which was statutorily required, it appears that Widecombe followed the law quite closely.

The dependency of the working population on poor relief is also partly a result of the fact that employment must have been seasonal, insecure and with no automatic provision if you fell ill or were injured or otherwise incapacitated. Also the level of wages probably allowed very little to be stashed away for just such times. It was certainly a hand to mouth existence for the casual labourer and the poor relief system was a vital and important fall-back for all those in work as well as for those who could not work for one reason or another.

A reasonable conclusion from the evidence presented here would be that the poor of Widecombe seem to have been a lot better off than the general urban poor, who appear from the literature to have had a pretty raw deal. This may be because the poor in Widecombe were fewer in number and therefore more manageable than those in urban settings. It may also be the case that everyone no doubt knew everyone else in Widecombe and so perhaps there were elements of the 'extended family' in operation in the community support that was provided, again something that may not have applied to those in urban situations. Furthermore, both the fact that the scattered settlements of the rural parish of Widecombe had a spiritual centre in the church at Widecombe, and that there was also a building that could be used to accommodate the poor with nowhere else to go (the Church House), were undoubtedly also factors in the success of the provision of relief in Widecombe.

Of course, it is important to define what is meant here by 'welfare'. It could be interpreted quite broadly or quite narrowly and it is true that the primary focus of the present volume is on the relatively narrow provision of poor relief, whether that be in terms of payment for relief, or work assigned and carried out, or in terms of clothing supplied, or in terms of medical help provided, and even payment for burial. However, it is also true to say that the church provided spiritual welfare for the bulk of the population, poor and rich alike and those in-between, and so some discussion of that has been included here. And, although it might be seen to be stretching the definition somewhat, the maintenance of the local highways might also be considered welfare in that good care of the highways assists the ability of the parishioners to move freely about the parish. And we must not forget the importance of education for the young and the prevalence of the apprenticeship system. These are all benefits that we take for granted today even though we pay towards them through our national and local taxes and rates, but clearly there was a need to provide them even then, and, because it was organised at a local parish level, we have the records to show what went on and it is that story that is told in these pages.

WIDECOMBE-IN-THE-MOOR

The village of Widecombe-in-the-Moor (Widecombe for short) is located in eastern Dartmoor in Devon, south-west England and lies about 10 kilometres both from Ashburton to the south-east and Bovey Tracey to the east. It is at an elevation of approximately 250 meters above sea level, which usually results in a temperature reduction of about 2 degrees Celsius compared to the surrounding lowlands. Even though it is nestled in a valley it is very much 'in-the-Moor' and it is often subject to severe moorland weather and quite significant rainfall. It can be beautiful too!

FIGURE 1-2: WIDECOMBE-IN-THE-MOOR VILLAGE NESTLED IN THE WIDECOMBE VALLEY LOOKING WEST (IMAGE COPYRIGHT THE AUTHOR).

The village is only a small part of a large parish of just over 4,290 hectares, of which 1860 hectares are open moorland.[1] It had a population of 974 according to the 1851 census, with most settlement being relatively remote and scattered. Poundsgate is the largest hamlet outside of Widecombe itself, with others including Dunstone, Venton, Ponsworthy and Lowertown.

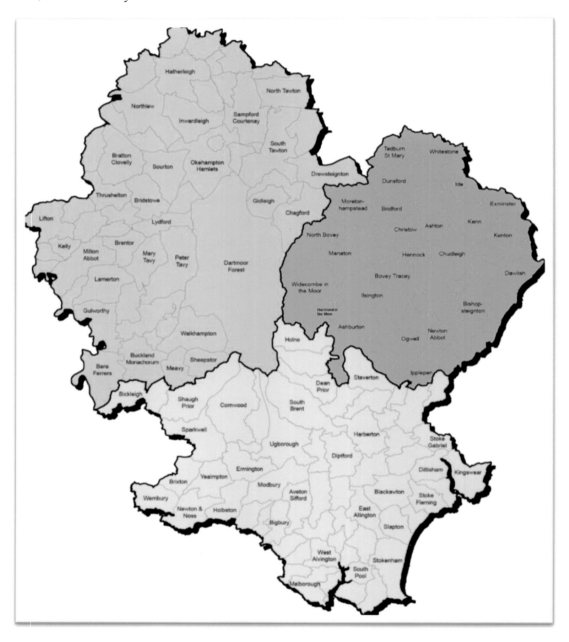

FIGURE 1-3: TEIGNBRIDGE, SOUTH-HAMS AND WEST DEVON PARISHES SHOWING WIDECOMBE-IN-THE-MOOR

(IMAGE COPYRIGHT DEVON BUILDING CONTROL (WEBSITE: DEVONBUILDINGCONTROL.GOV.UK) USED WITH PERMISSION)

---

[1] See Widecombe-in-the-Moor Conservation Area Character Appraisal available at http://www.dartmoor.gov.uk/__data/assets/pdf_file/0005/865409/Widecombe-2011.pdf.

Introduction

Figure 1-3 shows Widecombe Parish very much in the heart of south-central Devon with Dartmoor Forest immediately to the west and Buckland-in-the-Moor cradled to the south-east. The Forest Quarter as referred to in this book is the section of the Forest adjacent to the boundary with Widecombe[2].

FIGURE 1-4: WIDECOMBE PARISH AND SURROUNDING AREA WITH PARISH BOUNDARY OUTLINED IN RED FROM THE NEW POPULAR EDITION ORDNANCE SURVEY MAPS (1945-8)

(IMAGE COPYRIGHT OLIVER, R.R., KAIN, R.J.P., REPRODUCED WITH PERMISSION)

Figure 1-4 shows Widecombe-in-the-Moor parish and its immediate surrounding area as shown by the Ordnance Survey one inch to the mile (1:63,360) New Popular Edition maps (1945-8) overlaid with the parish boundaries shown as a solid red line[3].

---

[2] See Figure 13-1 for a map of the Forest Quarter.

[3] This map is taken, with permission, from Oliver, R. R., Kain, R. J. P. (2001). Historic Parishes of England and Wales: an Electronic Map of Boundaries before 1850 with a Gazetteer and Metadata. [data collection]. UK Data Service. SN: 4348, http://doi.org/10.5255/UKDA-SN-4348-1.

Historic Ordnance Survey maps are viewable in full, along with other maps, at the excellent National Library of Scotland website at maps.nls.uk.

Many of the places mentioned in the text can be identified on the map in Figure 1-4, including some of the tenements in the Forest Quarter to the west of Widecombe such as Huccaby, Hexworthy and Pizwell.

You can find out more about Widecombe by visiting https://widecombe-in-the-moor.com.

THE WIDECOMBE DIGITAL ARCHIVE PROJECT

The inspiration for this book originated with the Widecombe History Group project to digitise the documents preserved in the Widecombe Parish Chest that began in 2011. There was a wealth of detail hidden away in these documents and although the challenge of making these documents available to a wider audience was daunting, a team of volunteers methodically worked their way through the chest contents, scanning and cataloguing each page of every document. The Parish Chest contents were all digitised by 2014 and since then the team has continued to digitise the History Group's own expanding archive, as well as items loaned by local residents. So many snippets of stories of the lives of Widecombe folk popped out from these documents that it seemed essential to attempt to bring these to a wider audience and this book is one result of that. We hope you enjoy reading this book and that you will be encouraged to investigate further into some of the stories included here and discover others for yourself.

CHAPTER 2 BACKGROUND AND CONTEXT

FIGURE 2-1: WIDECOMBE VILLAGE WITH ST. PANCRAS CHURCH IN THE CENTRE AND THE CHURCH HOUSE ON THE RIGHT (PARTIALLY OBSCURED BY A TREE)

(IMAGE COPYRIGHT THE AUTHOR)

Poor relief in Britain has from the earliest times been perceived as the duty of the Christian Church and originally it would have been provided in some way from the tithes that were collected and divided between the Church, the vicar or incumbent, the maintenance of the parish church fabric and the relieving of the poor.

Sidney and Beatrice Webb quote the following passage[4] from the ordinance ascribed in the eighth century to Egbert, Archbishop of York:

> *"The priests are to take the tithes of the people,......The first part they are to take for the adornment of the church; but the second ....to distribute with their own hands, for the use of the poor and strangers; the third part, however, the priests may reserve for themselves."*

Over time, due perhaps in part to the various entitlements to tithes being sold on and/or ownership changing, these supplementary purposes began to be lost and looking after the church fabric and relieving the poor became separated off from the

---

[4] Webb, 1927, on page 2.

tithe and as a result separate and quite distinct sums of money were raised for these purposes via a Church Rate and a Poor Rate.

Again, from Webb[5]:

> *"Already by the twelfth century, it seems, the tithe had ceased to supply any appreciable sum towards the relief of the poor. The high dignitaries of the Church, the alien priories, the various conventual or collegiate bodies in England itself and lay impropriators gradually got into their hands most of the well-endowed benefices, or the greater part of their tithes; and in spite of repeated injunctions, and even statutory provisions, it seems clear that, by the end of the fifteenth century, at any rate, these absentee proprietors made no regular subventions for the poor of the parishes whence their revenues were derived."*

Thus, in Widecombe's case, close examination reveals that the Churchwardens' Accounts reflect the Church Rate being collected, and the Overseers' Accounts likewise reflect the collection of the Poor Rate. It may be that the amount of tithes collected by the church was reduced as a result of these separate rates also being collected, although no direct evidence of this has been found.

It is also easy to forget that the enforcement of the Poor Law was the responsibility of the Justices of the Peace and that they themselves were subject (in varying degrees) to supervision from above. Thus we see in 1597 the Devon Justices receiving an order from their Lord Lieutenant to be stirred to more energetic action to see that the statutes relating to vagrants and the relief of the impotent poor were universally enforced[6].

Whatever the cause it is the case that additional legislation to provide for the poor became more and more common, culminating in the acts of 1597-1601, towards the end of the reign of Elizabeth I, which were in part a consequence of a period in English history when conditions for the manual working class had become particularly bad. Then, in 1601, it was the passing of another Act which, although basically a refinement of the 1597 Act and a consolidation of previous legislation[7], is normally credited as the starting point of the Old Poor Laws. Under this Act, each parish was obliged to relieve the aged and the helpless, to raise vulnerable children in trades such as farming, and to provide work for those capable of it but who couldn't find it for themselves for whatever reason.

---

[5] Webb 1927, page 3.

[6] Ibid., page 71.

[7] For instance, the 1563 Act for the Relief of the Poor had already provided, amongst other things, that those who refused to contribute to poor relief could be bound over to the Justice of the Peace and fined.

As a result of this 1601 Act:

- The parish became the administrative unit responsible for poor relief, with Churchwardens or parish Overseers collecting poor-rates and allocating relief.
- Materials of a suitable nature were to be made available to provide work for the able-bodied poor. Any able-bodied pauper who refused to work was subject to penalties.
- The parish was also responsible for the relief of the truly vulnerable poor - those who were aged, incapacitated, incapable of work, and so on. This could include the provision of almshouses as places for them to live. In Widecombe part of the Church House fulfilled this function. Although the relief and maintenance of such persons was made the legal responsibility of their relatives this was only if such relatives were themselves able to provide this support.
- The parish was also charged with the setting to work and apprenticeship of children.

The collection of the poor rate was carried out by the parish Overseers who were unpaid and elected annually by the parish vestry. This was understandably never a popular job but had to be done, and in Widecombe the accounts show the Overseers changing each year with no apparent difficulty. The Poor Rate was dispensed to the needy of the parish as 'out-relief', usually in the form of bread, clothing, fuel, the payment of rent, and/or money. In Widecombe it seems to have been dispensed mainly as clothing and money, with occasional food distributions. More detail is provided of how the money was spent in Chapter 7 - Providing for the Poor.

THE POOR RATE

Various acts prior to 1601 had empowered parish Overseers to raise money for poor relief from the inhabitants of the parish[8], according to their ability to pay.

In Widecombe the farms and landed estates were the main providers according to the lists in the Overseers' Accounts and it seems to have been the occupier who paid rather than the owner, since many farms were owned by absentee landlords. The amount of money raised varied from year to year and was generally as much as was necessary to balance the books. The Overseers would determine how much they needed and raise the rate accordingly. Sometimes more than one rate was raised in a year. Although this process was embodied in the 1601 Act, it is likely that some similar system was already in place in Widecombe. There was a 'Deed of the Customs' in the parish chest that recorded the agreement between the tithe payers

---

[8] e.g. the 1563 Act noted above.

and the vicar as to how the tithe should be paid. No mention is made of poor rate in this document, but it would not be hard to imagine that something similar was in place. And Widecombe in general would have been a reasonably well-off place at that time with both farming and tin production being the main industries (given that the church tower was supposedly built with money provided by local tin miners and the cost of repairing the tower and the church after the great storm of 1638 must have been substantial).

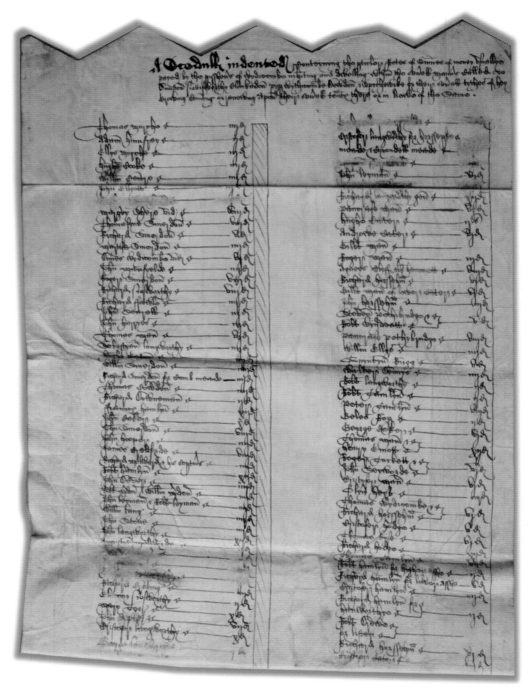

FIGURE 2-2: SOME OF THE SIGNATORIES TO THE 1586 DEED OF THE CUSTOMS

(IMAGE A041.P003 FROM THE WIDECOMBE ARCHIVE)

THE GILBERT ACT

There were various relatively small adjustments that took place to the Poor Laws during the 1600s and 1700s, but the first major change occurred in the 1780s with the Gilbert Act 'for the Better Relief and Employment of the Poor'[9]. This Act provided for the upgrade and improvements to the workhouse and also the appointment of salaried governors or governesses. Details of the effect of this Act on Widecombe will be found in Chapter 7 Providing for the Poor: The Poorhouse or Workhouse.

1830S MAJOR OVERHAUL

The 1832 Royal Commission conducted a detailed survey of the state of poor law administration in England and prepared a lengthy report. This report took the (typically Victorian?) view that poverty was essentially caused by the indigence of individuals rather than economic and social conditions that were outside their control. In consequence the report concluded that the pauper claimed relief regardless of his (or her) merits; large families got most, which encouraged improvident marriages; women claimed relief for bastard children, which encouraged immorality; labourers had no incentive to work; and employers kept wages artificially low as workers were subsidised from the Poor Rate.

The Commission published its report in March 1834 and made a series of recommendations which were to form the basis of the new legislation that followed in the same year. Its main proposal was that apart from medical attendance, and subject to the exception of apprenticeship, all relief whatever to able-bodied persons or to their families, otherwise than in well-regulated workhouses shall be declared unlawful, and shall cease; and that all relief afforded in respect of children under the age of 16 shall be considered as afforded to their parents.

In addition, it recommended:

- The grouping of parishes for the purposes of operating a workhouse
- That workhouse conditions should be 'less desirable' than those that an independent labourer of the lowest class could enjoy (the so-called 'workhouse test')
- That a central body should be appointed to administer the new system

These recommendations show quite a different attitude to poverty in general and the aged and infirm in particular than hitherto (although those with medical reasons appear to be exempted from the provisions). In Widecombe's case it meant that

---

[9] 22nd George the Third c 83 - see Webb 1927, page 272.

those who were the 'In' poor[10] would be administered under a group workhouse system, what would become known as the Newton Abbot Union.[11] Also the task of the Overseers was replaced by that of the more centralised 'Guardians of the Poor'. Although the Poor Rate continued to be collected, it was carried out by different collectors.

THE WORKHOUSE

The provision of a properly run workhouse must have been an expensive business, especially if there was no suitable local building. In Webb 1927[12] it is incidentally reported (in the Second Report from the House of Commons Committee on Poor Laws 1818) that in Devon in 1808, out of 473 parishes, 103 have workhouses, with the proportion being lowest in the moorland districts. We know that Widecombe was fortunate to have the Church House, a substantial building, available and in use (at least partly) as a workhouse at that date[13]. We also know that according to the episcopal visitations record, that there was an almshouse in Widecombe in 1744.[14] These visitations also indicate that there was no workhouse in Buckland, Holne or Manaton (all neighbouring parishes to Widecombe). It would appear also that there was no workhouse in Lydford parish although the visitation report is not explicit on this point.

In 1814 the workhouse in Widecombe was being upgraded and 'fitted out' to accommodate new rules governing their conduct. Salaried governesses were appointed, and a standardised diet was adopted. This is discussed in more detail in Chapter 7.

THE TYPES OF 'POOR'

In a place like Widecombe, a largely rural farming community, it seems reasonable to think that there would have been sufficient employment opportunities in farming husbandry albeit as an unskilled and perhaps seasonal farm labourer. What is less clear, of course, is how sufficient the pay for this type of work would have been, especially for looking after a family. Even so, it can be imagined that those

---

[10] See more on the types of poor below - 'In' poor are those living within the workhouse as opposed to the 'Out' poor who are living elsewhere.

[11] See Chapter 10 on the Newton Abbot Union for more details.

[12] page 215.

[13] A fair assumption on the basis that the workhouse facilities were being upgraded by 1814.

[14] see Appendix C.

who were poor and unable to find work, or to be provided with work, must have been largely unemployable, either through age, infirmity, illness or other incapacity. So we can perhaps attempt to classify the categories of the poor to enable us to better understand those who might have been subject to poor relief. These break down into two types:

- 'In' poor - those who were living 'in' the workhouse
- 'Out' poor - those who were living in the community

And those two types might be poor for a number of reasons, such as:

- They might be permanently or temporarily sick and unable to work
- They might be incapacitated (e.g. disabled or mentally ill)
- They might be 'with BC' (Bastard or Base Child)
- They might be elderly (no state pension of course)
- They might be bone-idle. However, it is not sure if there were any who fell into this category in Widecombe.
- They might be from other parishes and be provided for within Widecombe, perhaps on a temporary basis.

The above list comprises mainly people who could not work even if work was available. There were also those, perhaps the majority, perhaps not, who *could* work and were provided with work by the Overseers. There is certainly evidence of regular payments of money by the Overseers to the poor (as evidenced by the Overseers' Accounts), but it is less clear if work was done in exchange.

Finally, we must not forget those who were poor (of whatever type), that were being provided for in the community, either by their families, or their employers, or by those who somehow felt a responsibility, whether from some filial, or otherwise long-standing relationship. This might especially be the case, for instance, for some elderly poor who worked for a farmer and have since become too old or infirm, or the wife of such a worker where the worker has passed away. One can imagine many other similar circumstances and that not all farmers would cast such long-standing employees out once they had passed beyond working age.

THE LAW OF SETTLEMENT AND REMOVAL

With the Poor Law's requirement that the poor of a parish should be relieved through the raising of money from the local community, it seems sensible that there would be a parallel set of laws limiting the liability of a parish to ensure that it is not expending money on someone who does not belong to them. The 1662 Law of Settlement and Removal did that by ensuring that there was a system in place to remove persons from a parish who did not belong there. This led to a severe set of restrictions on travel for those who were not of the propertied classes. The comparative sense of security provided by 'belonging' to a parish was offset by the opposite feeling if you found yourself elsewhere.

Webb, once again[15], summed up this feeling of security:

> *"Every person was, as serf or as freeman, a member of some local community, to which he owed obligations, and from which he was entitled to expect some measure of protection, and, when in need, some undefined support."*

And the opposite[16]:

> *"An unknown person, absent without credentials from the community to which he belonged, was an object of grave suspicion."*

Once again, the reader is referred to Webb for a full account of this process including an account of some of the measures taken to prevent 'foreigners' from gaining residence in the parish, since there was a set of rules by which someone could become so resident. And what of those who did not have a 'home' parish or had forfeited that right through their travels? One can imagine a person or family falling out with the local Overseers and trying their luck elsewhere. This began to get much more difficult to achieve.

It does not take very much to imagine the hardships that could have ensued. The process of removal of an individual and/or family by the Overseers was a legal one and therefore had to be carried out in the right way through a process of interviews (or 'Examinations') and Removal Orders. Often these would involve additional investigations such as travelling to the stated 'home' parish and discussing the matter there. As a result, we find in the Widecombe parish records that there are over one hundred Examinations and approximately forty Removal Orders, all from the 1800s. It is likely that there were many more prior to that date but these are currently lost to us.

---

[15] Webb 1927, page 315.

[16] Ibid., page 315.

CHAPTER 3 THE WIDECOMBE TITHE AND RATES SYSTEM

FIGURE 3-1: TYTHE IN KIND; OR THE SOW'S REVENGE.

ETCHING FROM THE WIT'S MAGAZINE, I. 41 FROM MARCH 1784 (© TRUSTEES OF THE BRITISH MUSEUM)

The tithe system is, for the most part, outside the scope of this study, since, by the time period covered here (1700-1900), the tithes had long been removed from any connection with poor relief[17]. It had also been removed, other than indirectly, from the raising of money for church matters, including repairs. Its relevance here really only lies in the correspondence between those who paid tithes and those who paid the Church and Poor Rates, which generally speaking were the same. This can be seen partly from the 1805 Overseers' Accounts where both the vicar and Lord Ashburton, who owned some rectorial tithes, paid Poor Rates on their tithe

---

[17] As per Webb, 1927, on page 3 and mentioned in Chapter 2 above.

receipts[18]. Interestingly, they did not pay the Church Rate on these holdings, although, in most other respects, and for almost all the other holdings, the monies raised match very closely.

The Widecombe Deed of the Customs (now at the SW Heritage Trust Devon Archives) defined the agreement (at least in 1586 and beyond) between the vicar and local landowners and occupiers as to how tithes would be paid in Widecombe, with many 'in kind' tithes replaced by monetary equivalents. This was signed by 93 local landowners and occupiers (see Figure 2-2).[19]

It is possible that this agreement formed the basis on which the Widecombe land holdings were valued at that time (and subsequently) for general rating purposes and that the Poor Rate and other rates would have been calculated in more or less the same way. For instance the Church Rate and the Poor Rate were always determined as an amount of money in the pound, so if the rateable value of a holding was, say, £5 and the rate being raised was at one shilling in the pound then the landowner or occupier of the holding would pay five shillings. It would also seem reasonable (in general) that if one occupier paid twice as much tithe as another then they would also pay twice as much Poor Rate and Church Rate. It seems unlikely that there was a different underlying rateable value for each type of rate since the amounts that were collected could easily be varied by changing the rate in the pound that was being raised. Having said that, there were no doubt individual negotiations to try to limit the amounts paid.

This system provides, in effect, a rateable value (in modern day terms) for each holding that can used to calculate the amount of rates and other property-based taxes that are due. As land changed hands for one reason or another, so the person paying the tithe or rate would change, although the total amount raised would stay the same.

There was also another extant document, that may or may not have been in the parish chest. This provided a list of those who had carried out the role of Churchwarden (a transcript of this document is preserved as A060.002A). This also (mostly) listed the tenements in the parish (since the duty of providing a churchwarden was a commitment of the tenement rather than of an individual), and therefore may have acted as one of the lists of properties that were subject to tax (or at least was derived from it). Some more detail is provided on this document in Chapter 4.

---

[18] See Appendix A. Also Evans 1976 page 31 notes that tithes were rated to 'land tax, property tax, income tax (after 1799) and, most important of all, poor rates'.

[19] This is, of course, an extremely complex topic. A good coverage of the problems faced by payers and receivers of tithes can be found in 'The Contentious Tithe' - see bibliography.

So far, no evidence of a definitive master list of properties and values has been found, although a list of tithes collected in 1813 for Widecombe has been located in the Exeter Cathedral Archive[20], which looks similar, although not quite the same as the Churchwardens' and Overseers' Accounts lists. It is possible, therefore, that all of these money collectors acted more or less independently of one another.

For comparison purposes, the 1813 tithe list referred to above indicates that £2 6s was collected from Dockwell. This compares to the 1803-4 Poor Rate collection of 9s, which however is collected fourfold in that year (amounting to £1 16s in all) and the 1803-4 Church Rate collection of 1s 6d. The equivalent figures for Chittleford are £8 7s for the Tithe, £1 9s 3d for a single Poor Rate and 4s 6d for a single Church Rate.

A completely new tithe list was produced as a result of the 1836 Tithe Commutation Act and this is available for study as it relates to Widecombe in the form of the Tithe Apportionment Register[21] and the accompanying Tithe Map that resulted from that process, both safely stored at the SW Heritage Trust Devon Archives.

Further reading on the English Tithe system is provided in the bibliography for those that want to delve deeper. Figure 3-1 shows a satirical illustration from 1784 highlighting the contentious nature of the tithe system, with the parson, who of course has to be fat and well-fed, being attacked by a sow after he has arrived to assess the tithable goods of the land occupier. The parson is lucky that the pig-house yard area is so clean!

INTERESTING ASIDE 1: THE USE OF 'J' AT THE END OF AMOUNTS IN THE 1586 DEED OF THE CUSTOMS

Since the Middle Ages, a "j" has sometimes been substituted for the final "i" of a lower- or upper-case Roman numeral, such as "iij" for 3 or "vij" for 7. This was to prevent the value being changed. For example, VII could easily have been changed to VIII, but using VIJ prevents this happening.[22]

---

[20] Under Exeter Cathedral Archive reference 6037/18/1.

[21] Which can also be viewed online at https://widecombearchive.org.uk/tithe_apportionments.php.

[22] See https://www.answers.com/Q/What_is_the_value_of_j_as_a_Roman_numeral.

CHAPTER 4 WHO ADMINISTERED THE SYSTEM?

FIGURE 4-1: THOMAS ROWLANDSON (1757-1827): A SELECT VESTRY. 1806
(THE ELISHA WHITTELSEY COLLECTION, METROPOLITAN MUSEUM OF ART, PUBLIC DOMAIN)

THE CHURCHWARDENS AND OVERSEERS OF THE POOR

The primary local administrators of the rates system were the Overseers of the Poor and the Churchwardens, under the day to day control of the incumbent vicar or rector and answerable to the local Justices of the Peace.

The document referred to in the previous chapter (on page 16) that showed the tenements, farms and estates that had executed the role of Churchwarden, in many cases named the individual or individuals who carried out the role. The document may be missing but there is a transcript of it that was made by Robert Dymond in the 1800s. Or, to be more precise, there is a later typed copy of the handwritten transcript which is recorded in the Widecombe Archive under the catalogue number A060.002A (this is fortunate because the Robert Dymond transcript also appears to be missing).[23] The original document was produced in 1750, but includes details from 1660 onwards so was probably a replacement or consolidation of an even earlier document. It was maintained until about 1821. As well as listing individuals, it also provides a good idea of the tenements which had the obligation to provide a churchwarden and therefore probably also to pay tithes. The Churchwardens were appointed in rotation to ensure that the obligation was fairly spread. Once you had fulfilled your obligation as Churchwarden it was unlikely to come around again for some considerable time.

It is instructive to note some of the duties of the Churchwardens as recorded in 'The Compleat Parish Officer':

> *"Churchwardens are to see that the Parishioners come to Church every Sunday, and to present the Names of such who [are] absent, to the Ordinary; or levy 1s for every offence.[....] They are not to permit any to stand idle, walk or talk in the Church or Churchyard; to take Care that no persons sit in the Church with their Hats on, or in any other indecent Manner, but that they behave themselves orderly, soberly and reverently."[24]*

Overseers of the Poor were appointed annually from the parishioners to raise the Poor Rate and administer poor relief, and Churchwardens likewise for the maintenance of the fabric of the church and other church related duties (such as the supply of wine for the sacrament and paying for someone to look after and teach the singing - see Chapter 6 on the Church Rate). The Churchwardens were also responsible for the poor of the parish and worked with the Overseers in setting the Poor Rate etc. These were onerous tasks and unpaid and therefore not very popular but had to be done. The officers had to meet at least monthly 'to consider of proper Methods for the Relief of and providing for the Poor'.[25]

---

[23] The full transcript of this document can be seen on the Widecombe Archive website by searching for A060.002A. This includes a pdf copy of the transcript.

[24] Church, 'The Compleat Parish Officer' page 43. According to this booklet, Compulsory Church attendance is recorded by Statute (1 Eliz. c.1.), and the other duties are recorded in the Church Canon 18 and 111.

[25] Ibid., page 58.

THE ACCOUNT BOOKS

Both Overseers and Churchwardens prepared annual accounts that recorded the transactions that they carried out, which had to be signed off by the Justices of the Peace.

In Widecombe the parish chest contained a number of Overseers' Accounts preserved in books covering the following years:

- Fragments of 1 volume 1683-1684
- 3 volumes 1700 - 1785
- 2 volumes 1799 - 1824
- 1 volume 1834 - 1836

No doubt there were accounts prior to 1683 and also for the other years up to 1700, but these are missing and may be lost to us completely. Similarly, the later dates are missing (although the local accounting role of the Overseers was abolished in 1834 as a result of the Poor Law Amendment Act, so we should not expect to see any after that date).

The parish chest also had Churchwardens' Accounts covering:

- 2 volumes 1712 - 1770
- 2 volumes 1803 - 1877

Again, no doubt, there were other years for which accounts were prepared, but the records have been lost to us, although of course they may well turn up at any time.

All of the above account books that were in the parish chest have been digitised and may be viewed online by visiting https://widecombearchive.org.uk and choosing the main Parish Archive. The direct link is:

https://www.widecombearchive.org.uk/main_archive.php

More details on using this Archive can be found in Appendix D.

The original documents are now in the safekeeping of South West Heritage Trust Devon Archives at the Exeter Record Office (website: https://swheritage.org.uk/devon-archives/)

The accounts were evidently drawn up at the end of the year as a reasonably fair copy (there are very few mistakes!!), so there would no doubt have been other, less formal, records maintained during the year that would have been used as the basis for these accounts. An amount of cash was usually brought forward from the year before from the previous Overseers and Churchwardens and the residual balance at the end of the year was likewise passed on to the next. There would also have been dockets, receipts etc., recording the various transactions. All of this supporting information is lost and may in fact not have been preserved once the annual

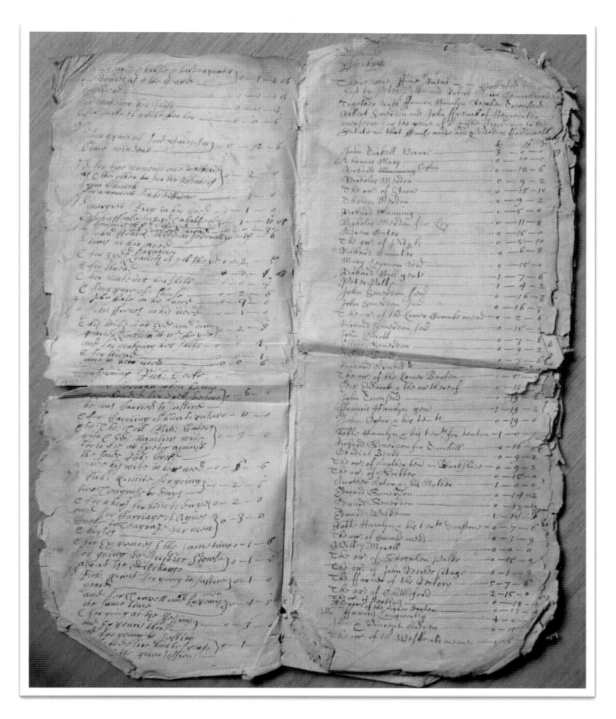

FIGURE 4-2: DOUBLE PAGE OF THE FRAGMENT OF THE OVERSEERS' ACCOUNT BOOK FROM 1683
(IMAGE A008.002 FROM THE WIDECOMBE ARCHIVE)

accounts had been signed off and the residual balance handed over to the next persons responsible.

The amount of money that was raised each year as a Poor or Church Rate varies, presumably as the anticipated expenditure fluctuates. For example, in 1805 a Church Rate of 'three half pence' (i.e. one and a half pence) in the pound was raised. This collected a total of £11-9-7½d from the landowners/occupiers. More information on this will be found in 'Raising the Church Rate' below.

It is also interesting that the phrase "to be Collected as Often as Need Shall Require" is used generally throughout these and the Overseers' Accounts. This indicates that if the expenditure should suddenly increase in an unpredictable way (e.g. through a natural cause such as a major storm damaging the church roof), the Churchwardens could raise a further rate and charge the parishioners accordingly.

In the same year (1805) there was a large Poor Rate charged (thirteen and a half pence in the pound). See Figure 4-3:

FIGURE 4-3: DETAIL FROM THE OVERSEERS' ACCOUNT BOOK FROM 1805

(IMAGE A006.006.P023 FROM THE WIDECOMBE ARCHIVE)

This rate yielded £317 17s 11d, a not inconsiderable sum.

We look in more detail at this sum and what it was spent on in Chapter 7 - Providing for the Poor.

THE SELECT VESTRY

The select vestry is to be contrasted with the general or open vestries. Whereas the open vestry was open to all ratepayers in a parish, the select vestry was an 'elected' group of individuals, taken from the ratepayers. The select vestries were eventually regulated by various Acts of Parliament, most notably in 1818[26] and this probably explains why the select vestry minutes of proceedings starts soon after that date. Figure 4-4 shows the establishment of the select vestry in Widecombe. It looks as if there had not been one before this date (and no document recording proceedings before this date has been found) but we do not, of course, know that for certain. In Widecombe those who acted on the select vestry appear to have been elected at a general vestry meeting once a year, as shown in the minute book and as shown in Figure 4-4 where the initial members of that vestry were elected by *the whole of the meeting then present*. The vicar generally acted as the chairman of the vestry meetings.

What the select vestry minutes do is show some of the decisions that were made regarding poor relief before they were ultimately reflected in the Overseers' Accounts. They do not always state *why* a particular decision was taken (for instance there are numerous references to pay being reduced but no statement as to why the reduction is being made). There is also no mention of the setting of the poor relief rate amount. How this was decided remains unclear, although it may be as simple as the Overseers stating how much they needed, and a simple calculation was then carried out to work out the rate needed to raise it. However, it seems unlikely that parishioners would accept this and so it would be expected that, for instance, the Justices of the Peace might well have sanctioned the amount, although no evidence of this has been found so far (other than by signing of the accounts after they have been prepared).

---

[26] for instance, the 'Act for the Regulation of Parish Vestries' (Vestries Act 1818, 58 Geo. III c. 69).

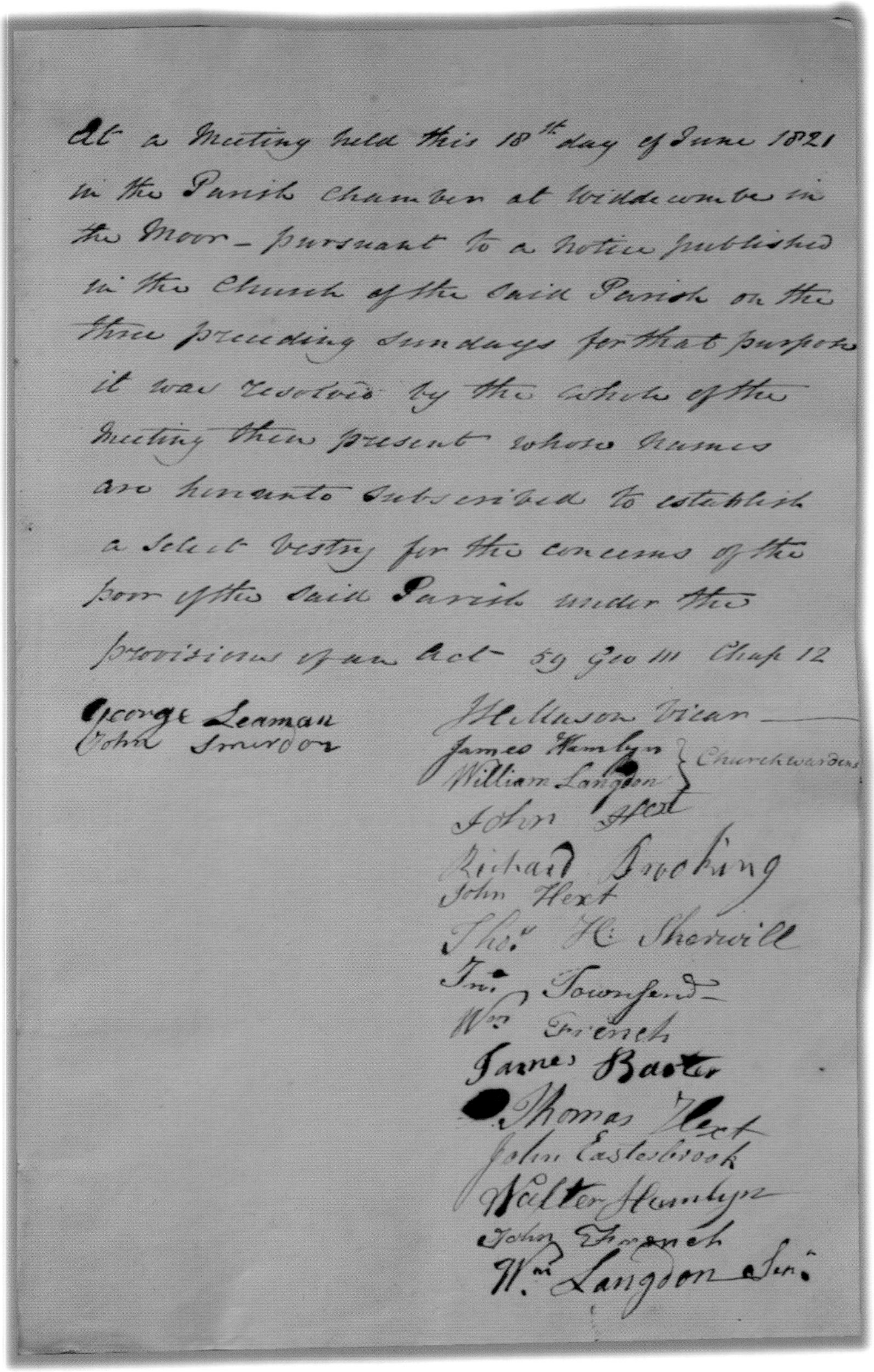

At a Meeting held this 18th day of June 1821 in the Parish chamber at Widdecombe in the Moor — pursuant to a notice published in the Church of the said Parish on the three preceding Sundays for that purpose it was resolved by the whole of the Meeting then present whose names are hereunto Subscribed to establish a Select Vestry for the concerns of the poor of the said Parish under the provisions of an act 59 Geo III Chap 12

George Leaman
John Smerdon

J Hillason Vicar
James Hamlyn   } Churchwardens
William Langdon }
John Hext
Richard Brooking
John Hext
Thos. H. Sherrill
Ini. Townsend
Wm French
James Baxter
Thomas Hext
John Easterbrook
Walter Hamlyn
John French
Wm Langdon Seni.

FIGURE 4-4: PAGE FROM THE WIDECOMBE SELECT VESTRY MINUTE BOOK RECORDING THE ESTABLISHMENT OF A SELECT VESTRY ON 18TH JUNE 1821

(DOCUMENT 2955A/PV/1 FROM THE SW HERITAGE TRUST DEVON ARCHIVES)

Who Administered the System?

The transcription of the document in Figure 4-4 is as follows:

At a Meeting held this 18th day of June 1821 in the Parish chamber at Widdicombe in the Moor - pursuant to a Notice published in the Church of the said Parish on the three preceding Sundays for that purpose it was resolved by the whole of the Meeting then present whose Names are hereunto subscribed to establish a Select Vestry for the concerns of the poor of the said Parish under the provisions of an Act 59 Geo III Chap 12

George Leaman JH Mason Vicar
John Smerdon   James Hamlyn}
                William Langdon} Churchwardens
                John Hext }
                Richard Brooking
                John Hext
                Thos H Sherwill
                Jno Townsend
                Wm French
                James Barter
                Thomas Hext
                John Easterbrook
                Walter Hamlyn
                John French
                Wm Langdon Senr

CHAPTER 5 THE WIDOW'S GIFT AND OTHER PRIVATE PROVISIONS

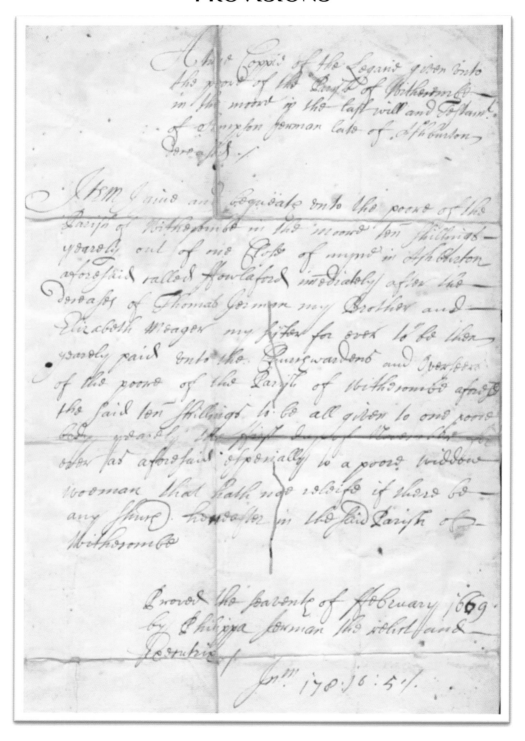

FIGURE 5-1: EXTRACT FROM THE WILL OF SAMSON JERMAN DATED 1669 RECORDING THE LEGACY TO BE GIVEN ANNUALLY TO A WIDOW FROM WIDECOMBE

(IMAGE A069.003.001 FROM THE WIDECOMBE ARCHIVE)

As well as the legal requirement to pay Poor and other rates, there were also other voluntary donations and bequests, as well as specific fund-raising activities such as the raising of subscriptions for the setting up of schools to provide basic education for the poor.[27]

There are also some specific bequests mentioned in the accounts that are worth highlighting here.

THE WIDOW'S GIFT

There is a document[28] preserved in the Widecombe Parish Chest recording what has become known as the Widow's Gift (see Figure 5-1):

This document reads as follows (as close as we can determine and using the original spellings etc):

A true Coppie of the Legacie given unto the poor of the Parish of Withecombe in the moore in the last will and Testam^t of Sampson Jerman late of Ashburton deceased ./.
Item I give and bequeath unto the poore of the Parish of Withecombe in the moore ten shillings yearely out of one Close of myne in Ashburton aforesaid called ffowlaford imediately after the deceases of Thomas Jerman my Brother and Elizabeth Meager my sister for ever to be then yearly paid unto the Churchwardens and Overseers of the poore of the Parish of Withecombe afores^d the said ten shillings to be all given to one poore lady yearly the ffirst day of November for ever as aforesaid especially to a poore widdow woman that hath noe releife if there be any shuch hereafter in the said Parish of Withecombe
Proved the seaventh of ffebruary 1669
by Philippa Jerman the relict and Executrix ./.
Jn^m 178:16:5 ./.

So from the death of Sampson's brother and sister onwards (forever! i.e. a perpetual lien over the plot of land called Fowlaford), there was to be an annual payment of 10 shillings received from whoever was the current owner of Fowlaford that would be paid to a woman, preferably a widow, in need *("that hath noe releife")*. Hence the name 'widow's gift' that has come to be associated with this bequest.

We can find reference to this payment in the Overseers' accounts (e.g. Figure 5-2).

---

[27] See Chapter 11 for more details on this.

[28] Widecombe Archive A069.

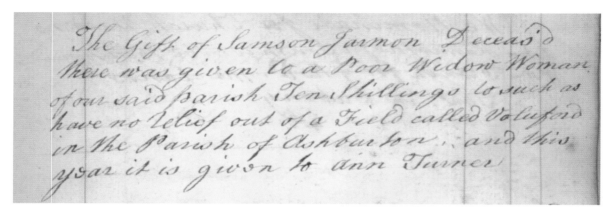

FIGURE 5-2: EXTRACT FROM THE OVERSEERS' ACCOUNT BOOK FROM 1805 SHOWING THE WIDOW'S GIFT
(IMAGE A006.006.P023 FROM THE WIDECOMBE ARCHIVE)

The transcription of the above is as follows:

The Gift of Samson Jarmon Deceas'd
there was given to a Poor Widow Woman
of our said parish Ten Shillings to such as
have no Relief out of a Field called Voluford
in the Parish of Ashburton and this
year it is given to Ann Turner

In the Report of the Commissioners concerning Charities[29], this annuity was still being paid. At the time the owner of the land was Sir Lawrence Palk, baronet.

The field name gradually changed to Goosepool, but the gift remained, and in 1947 there are documents in the archive showing Sylvia Sayer obtaining the ten shillings due from the then owner for the parish, as is their right! She also provides a list of all of the owners of the field from 1669 onwards taken from the deeds in the possession of that owner[30]. It is not known whether the Parish Council went on to claim the money and pay this sum to a local widow!

Of course, a *fixed* sum of ten shillings was specified, so the value of the bequest reduced over time as inflation bit into the value of the pound (although this might not have been noticeable until the twentieth century when inflation really took hold). On a retail price index basis, the equivalent would have been about £72 today, or just over £1,000 if average earnings were used as the measure[31].

---

[29] Vol IV dated 1830.

[30] Widecombe Archive A065.

[31] See the website measuringworth.com for a comprehensive guide to the change in the value of money and also Appendix F.

WHITE BREAD FOR THE POOR ON GOOD FRIDAY

There was another payment of a different type made in the 1734-35 accounts (see Figure 5-3):

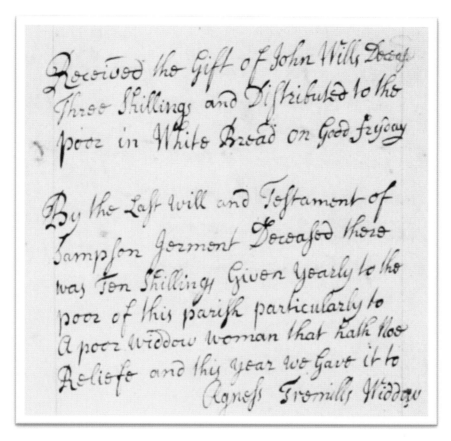

FIGURE 5-3: EXTRACT FROM THE OVERSEERS' ACCOUNT BOOK FROM 1734-5 SHOWING JOHN WILLS BEQUEST AND THE WIDOW'S GIFT

(IMAGE A003.P008 FROM THE WIDECOMBE ARCHIVE)

The transcription of Figure 5.3 is as follows:

Received the Gift of John Wills Deceasd
Three Shillings and Distributed to the
poor in White Bread on Good fryday

Also shown in the image and repeated out of interest mainly for the spelling differences and the writing style is the payment under the Widow's Gift:

By the Last Will and Testament of
of Sampson Jermont Deceased there
was Ten Shillings Given yearly to the
poor of this parish particularly to
A poor widdow woman that hath Noe
Reliefe and this year we Gave it to
Agness Tremills Widdow

CHAPTER 6 THE CHURCH RATE

FIGURE 6-1: THE NORTH SIDE OF THE CHURCH HOUSE TODAY

(IMAGE COPYRIGHT THE AUTHOR)

INTRODUCTION

In this chapter we consider the provisions for the maintenance of Widecombe Church both in terms of the fabric of the church and the maintenance of everything associated with providing regular church services. This is felt to be a legitimate part of welfare provision, especially during the 18th-19th centuries, when almost everyone went regularly to church. In addition, the Churchwardens' Accounts are themselves extremely interesting and enlightening, so it is well worth devoting a page or two to them.

The accounting year 1805 is examined as it forms a contrast to the study of the Overseers' Accounts for the same year.

Figure 6-1 shows the north side of the Church House, with the external staircases, one for girls and one for boys, clearly visible, both leading to what were the schoolrooms on the upper floor.

RAISING THE CHURCH RATE

The amount of money that was raised each year as a Poor or Church Rate varies, presumably as the anticipated expenditure fluctuates. For example in 1805 a church rate of three half pence in the pound was raised (see Figure 6-2).

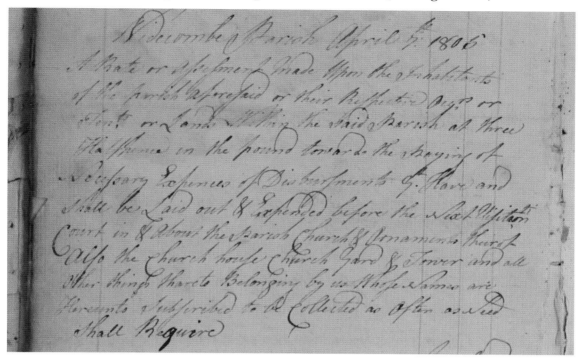

FIGURE 6-2: DETAIL FROM THE CHURCHWARDENS' ACCOUNT BOOK FROM 1805 SHOWING AGREEMENT TO RAISE THE CHURCH RATE

(IMAGE A023.P009 FROM THE WIDECOMBE ARCHIVE)

The transcription of the extract in Figure 6-2 is as follows with the line breaks matching:

Widecombe Parish April 7th 1805
A Rate or Assesment Made Upon the Inhabitants
of the parish aforesaid or their Respective Occ^{rs} or
Ten^{ts} or Lands Within the said parish at three
Halfpence in the pound towards the paying of
Necessary Expences of Disbursments [that] Have and
shall be Laid out & Expended before the Next Visitation
Court in & About the Parish Church & Ornaments theirof
Also the Church house Church Yard & Tower and all
Other things thereto Belonging by us Whose Names are
Hereunto Subscribed to be Collected as Often as Need
Shall Require

This indicated that £11 9s 7½d was to be collected from the landowners/occupiers as shown by the extract from the accounts in Figure 6-3. However, in fact the assessment was collected fourfold as evidenced in the summary at the end of the accounts and the total sum collected that year was £45 18s 6d.

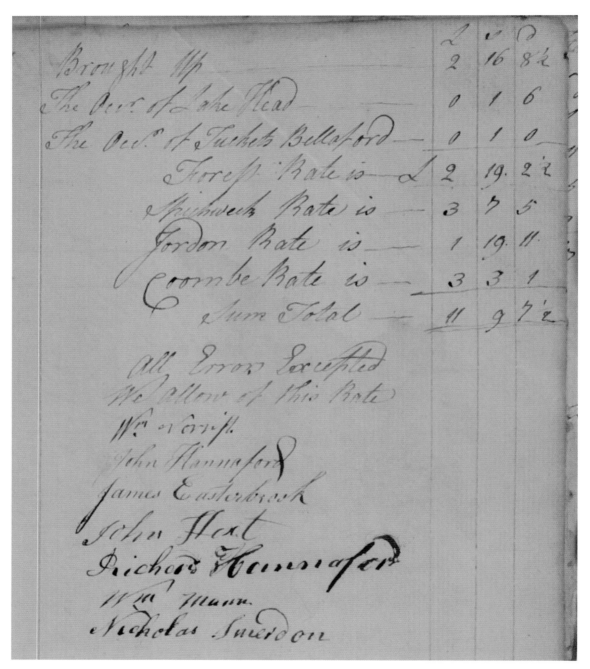

FIGURE 6-3: DETAIL FROM THE CHURCHWARDENS' ACCOUNT BOOK FROM 1805 SHOWING BASE AMOUNT RAISED

(IMAGE A023.P011 FROM THE WIDECOMBE ARCHIVE)

The transcription of the extract in Figure 6-3 is as follows:

	£	s	d
Brought Up	2	16	8 ½
The Occ^r of Lake Head	0	1	6
The Occ^r of Tuckets Bellaford	0	1	0
Forest Rate is -- £	2	19	2 ½
Spichweek Rate is	3	7	5
Jordon Rate is	1	19	11
Coombe Rate is	3	3	1
Sum Total	11	9	7 ½
All Errors Excepted			
We allow of this Rate			
Wm Norrish			
John Hannaford			
James Easterbrook			
John Hext			
Richard Hannaford			
Wm Mann			
Nicholas Smerdon			

It is worth mentioning at this point that the signatories in Figure 6-3 are all well-known local Widecombe names, many of whom are still common names in the area today.

As mentioned earlier, it is clear from this that all (or certain) properties must have had a rateable value that was similar to the one used today and this value was used as the basis for the rate calculation. This rateable value was also used for the raising of the Poor Rate.

Details of how to access a comprehensive transcript of the Churchwardens' Accounts for 1805 will be found in Appendix B.

RENTAL INCOME

In addition to the Church Rate, further income was obtained from the renting out of the Church House and other property in the ownership of the parish.

For instance, rent was received from a house in Dunstone owned by the parish (this was Lady House - according to A023.p013 – where there is an entry for thatch repair). There was also a meadow in Dunstone (Lady Meadow) which could be let separately or together with Lady House.

On 6th May 1805 a vestry meeting agreed that Church House rooms were to be let at £2 a year to John Tremills Junior for a school, viz. the Kitching Chamber, Little Fore Chamber and the School Chamber for the Purpose of Keeping School and the Linhay in the Back Court. (The room described as the School Chamber shows that the school must have already been established). See Figure 6-4 for the details.

Other rooms were let to Ann Smerdon also for 'keeping school'. These were the Parlour of the Church House and *"A Little Room Adjoining And part of the Wood House"* (see Figure 6-5).

A third set of rooms was let to John Potter, viz. *"the Kitching of the Church House, Little Back Chamber and the Little Foreroom and part of the Wood House"*. The purpose of this letting was not described but one wonders how many rooms there were in the Church House to be let in this way, and also if any rooms were used as a poor-house (see Figure 6-6).

All Church House lettings were at £2 per annum (present day income value £2,295).[32]

At some point during the latter part of the nineteenth century, the end rooms of the Church House were converted into a cottage for the Sexton. This would have reduced the space available to rent (and therefore for schooling) and may have occurred once the use of the Church House as an almshouse or workhouse had ceased.

The total income for 1805, from the Church Rate and rental etc., was £62 15s. One point worth noting here is that there is a strong correspondence between the list of Church Rate payers and the list of Poor Rate payers, as would be expected.[33] As was noted in Chapter 3, one notable difference is that those who received tithe payments paid Poor Rates on those receipts, but did not pay Church Rates.

---

[32] It is worth mentioning the practice of using Lady Day (March 25th in England) as the start date for many agreements. Up to 1752 it was the first day of the new year, so it has always had special significance. Search online if you are interested in finding out more.

[33] In fact, this was common practice, although without any statutory basis - see the Poor Law Commissioners Report on Local Taxation.

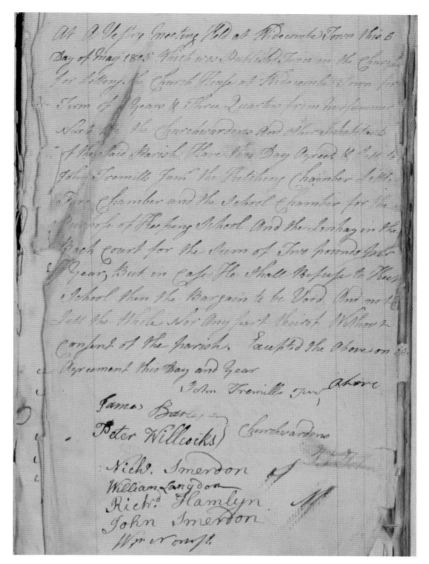

FIGURE 6-4: DETAIL FROM THE CHURCHWARDENS' ACCOUNT BOOK FROM 1805 CONCERNING LETTINGS
(IMAGE A023.P012 FROM THE WIDECOMBE ARCHIVE)

A partial transcript of Figure 6-4 is as follows:

*At a Vestry Meeting Held at Widecombe Town this 6
Day of May 1805 Which was Publishd Twice in the Church
for Letting the Church House at Widecombe Town for
Term of [..] Years & Three Quarters from Midsummer
Next [..] the Churchwardens and other Inhabitants
of the Said Parish Have this Day Agreed & Lett to
John Tremills Junr the Kitching Chamber Little
Fore Chamber and the School Chamber for the
Purpose of Keeping School And the Linhay in the
Back Court for the Sum of Two pounds per
Year, But in Case He Shall Refuse to Keep
School then the Bargain to be Void And not
Lett the Whole Nor Any part theirof Without
Consent of the parish*

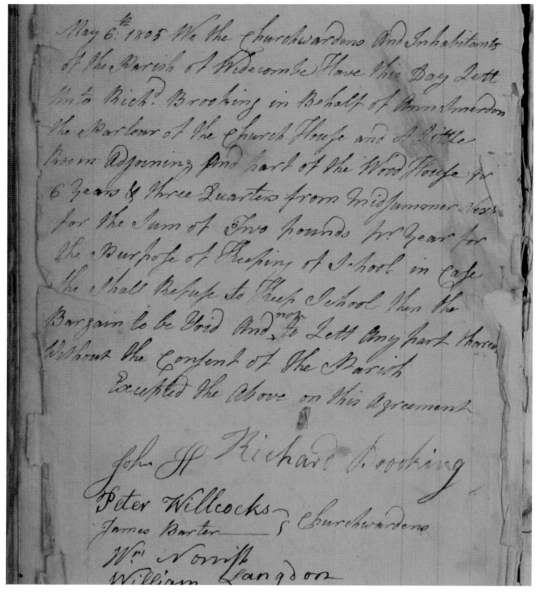

FIGURE 6-5: DETAIL FROM THE CHURCHWARDENS' ACCOUNT BOOK FROM 1805 SHOWING ANN SMERDON'S RENTAL

(IMAGE A023.P013 FROM THE WIDECOMBE ARCHIVE)

A partial transcript of Figure 6-5 is provided below:

May 6th 1805 We the Churchwardens And Inhabitants
of the Parish of Widecombe Have this Day Lett
Unto Richd Brooking in Behalf of Ann Smerdon
the Parlour of the Church House and A Little
Room Adjoining And part of the Wood House for
6 Years & three Quarters from Midsummer Next

for the Sum of Two pounds p^r Year for
the Purpose of Keeping of School

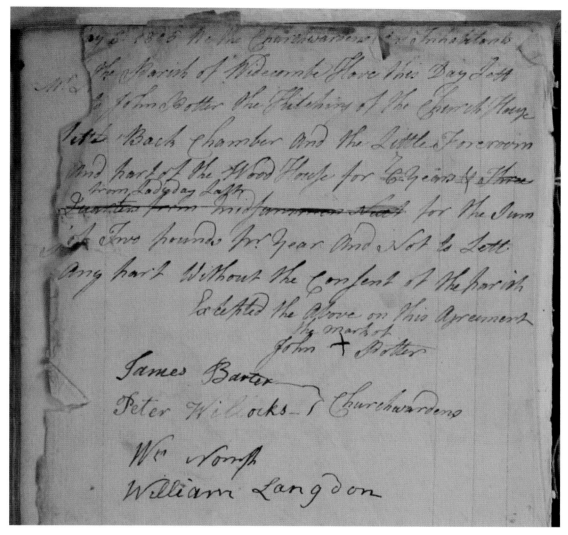

FIGURE 6-6: DETAIL FROM THE CHURCHWARDENS' ACCOUNT BOOK FROM 1805 SHOWING JOHN POTTER'S RENTAL

(IMAGE A023.P013 FROM THE WIDECOMBE ARCHIVE)

A partial transcript of Figure 6-6 is provided below (part of the original document is worn away or otherwise obscured):

[..]ay 6 1805 We the Churchwardens and Inhabitants
[..] The Parish of Widecombe Have this Day Lett
to John Potter the Kitching of the Church House
Little Back Chamber and the Little Foreroom
and part of the Wood House for 7 Years
from Ladyday Last
for the Sum
of Two Pounds p^r Year [...]

SPENDING THE CHURCH RATE

The expenditure that necessitated the raising of the Church Rate was an ongoing affair. Church and church building repairs might be small one year, but extensive the next and require local journeys of some distance to obtain the materials needed. There were also some regular costs incurred each year.

For instance, in 1805 there was the dinner laid on for the Minister which cost 5 shillings, and the dinner for the old and new Churchwardens, which cost 8 shillings. (About £30 in today's money for the Churchwardens' dinner - this might be considered to be fair enough given that they do the job without payment). These payments regularly appear in the accounts.

In addition to the dinners there was the Clerk's salary at £4 4s 0d and the Sexton's salary at £1 10s 0d. These sums are equivalent to £3,860 and £1,380 today using the index of average earnings.[34] Quite low but then perhaps they were not very onerous occupations and other work could have been taken on.

A Mr. Colander was paid for seventeen journeys to the parish for *"Instructing the Singing"*. This cost £8 18s 6d. Music in the church was a major attraction for all with both singing and instrumental accompaniment. It must have been quite exhilarating and, hopefully, entertaining.

There followed considerable items of expenditure on building materials, repairs etc to musical instruments and the bells (e.g. 3 shillings for *"New Hairing the Bow of the Bass Viol"*). There was then £5 10s 0d spent on 5 gallons of wine (quite a lot, but if it was used regularly for communion of the whole congregation then perhaps more understandable!), plus 5 shillings to transport the wine to Widecombe. There was also bread purchased for communion etc. Some of these items are shown in the extract below. The rest will be found in Appendix B.

---

[34] From www.measuringworth.com.

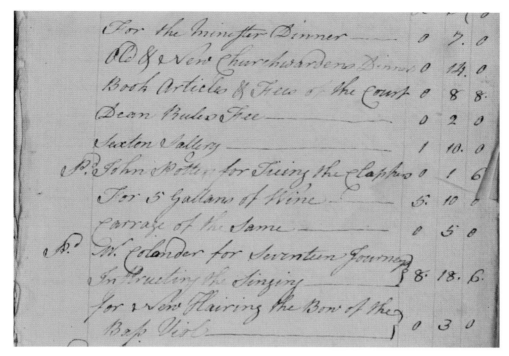

FIGURE 6-7: DETAIL FROM THE CHURCHWARDENS' ACCOUNT BOOK FROM 1805 SHOWING SOME EXPENDITURE

(IMAGE A023.P013 FROM THE WIDECOMBE ARCHIVE)

A transcript of the extract in Figure 6-7 is as follows:

For the Minester Dinner	0	7	0
Old & New Churchwardens Dinner	0	14	0
Book Articles & Fees of the Court	0	8	8
Dean Rules Fee	0	2	0
Sexton Sallery	1	10	0
P^d John Potter for Tieing the Clappers	0	1	6
For 5 Gallons of Wine	5	10	0
Carrage of the Same	0	5	0
P^d Mr Colander for Seventeen Journeys Instructing the Singing	8	18	6
for New Hairing the Bow of the Bass Viol	0	3	0

The outgoings for the year totalled £49 11s 0d, with the surplus of income over expenditure being passed on to the following year, as was usual.

Details of how to access a comprehensive transcript of the Churchwardens' Accounts for 1805 will be found in Appendix B. These transcripts provide much more detail on who the money was raised from and how it was spent.

CHAPTER 7 PROVIDING FOR THE POOR

FIGURE 7-1 : THOMAS ROWLANDSON (1757-1827): MEASURING SUBSTITUTES FOR THE ARMY OF RESERVE.
1815

(THE ELISHA WHITTELSEY COLLECTION, METROPOLITAN MUSEUM OF ART, PUBLIC DOMAIN)

INTRODUCTION

In this chapter we consider the various provisions for the poor of Widecombe and certain other matters that arise in the Overseers' Accounts. We will look at the raising of the money necessary to finance this poor provision and how it was spent.

Fundamentally it was the responsibility of the Overseers to administer this system, as discussed in Chapter 4, entitled 'Who Administered the System?'. The role of Overseer of the Poor was unpaid and ran for twelve months. Those undertaking the role were drawn from the local landowners and occupiers as was the case with the Churchwardens. The Overseers were responsible to the incumbent vicar and the Justices of the Peace and worked co-operatively with the Churchwardens in fulfilling their duties.

The year 1805 will again be used as an example.

RAISING THE MONEY FOR THE POOR

Money for the relief of the poor of Widecombe Parish was raised in various ways of which the main one, similar to the Church Rate, was through a Poor Rate which was levied on ratepayers according to statute and as described variously above in Chapters 2 and 4. The Poor Rate could be levied several times a year as necessary to meet the costs of dealing with the poor, which could be substantial at times. Ad hoc money was also raised, some through gifts or legacies (as noted in Chapter 5 above) and also from parishioners (e.g. maintenance for a child) and from other parishes (e.g. where the person is in Widecombe but is actually the responsibility of another parish - perhaps they are too ill to move).

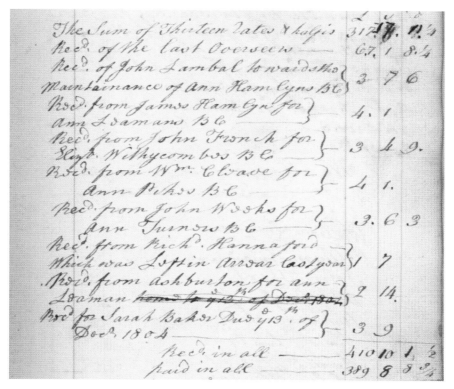

FIGURE 7-2: DETAIL FROM THE OVERSEERS' ACCOUNT BOOK FROM 1805 SHOWING MONEY RECEIPTS
(IMAGE A006.006.P023 FROM THE WIDECOMBE ARCHIVE)

The page shown in Figure 7-2 shows some of the monies received for the relief of the poor. There were some maintenance payments from men who had responsibility to a 'Bastard (or Base) Child' (BC as they were called). A partial transcript of Figure 7-2 is shown below.

Rec^d of John Lambal towards the Maintainance of Ann Hamlyns BC £3 7s 6d
Rec^d from James Hamlyn for Ann Leamans BC £4 1s
Rec^d from John French for Elizb Withycombes BC £3 4s 9d
Rec^d from Wm Cleave for Ann Pikes BC £4 1s
Rec^d from John Weeks for Ann Turners BC £3 6s 3d

Then there are a couple of new confinements prior to birth:

Rec^d from Ashburton for Ann Leaman home to ye 13th of Dec^t 1804 £2 14s
Rec^d for Sarah Baker Due ye 13th of Dec^t 1804 £3 9s

But the main regular money comes, of course, from the Poor Rate levied on the owners and occupiers of the farmsteads and estates in the parish. This rate was calculated slightly oddly. In the 1804/5 accounts *"treble poor rate at 3p in the £"* is declared. This yields £70 12s 10½d. This amount is then collected 4½ times, which makes a total collected of £317 17s 11d. So, *"the Sum of Thirteen Rates & halfes"* means that the amount of Poor Rate was collected at the rate of thirteen and a half pence in the pound, and this totalled £317 17s 11d, a not inconsiderable sum.[35]

As shown at the foot of Figure 7-2, with the other sums received the overall total of monies received was £410 10s 1½d. And the overall total of monies paid out in the year was £389 8s 8¾d. Any residual balance was carried forward from one year to the next.

A full transcript of the Overseers' Accounts for 1804/1805 is described in, and can be accessed from, Appendix A.

HOW WAS THE MONEY COLLECTED?

The 1572 Vagabonds Act[36] had legalised the levying of a local parish tax to raise funds for the provision of the poor. This was further consolidated in the 1601 Act.[37] These Acts gave the Overseers the power to levy rates and taxes on every inhabitant and occupier of houses, lands, tithes etc.

---

[35] See Appendix F for some discussion of the relative value of money between 1805 and today.

[36] 'An Act for the Punishment of Vagabonds, and for Relief of the Poor and Impotent' - see https://www.parliament.uk/about/living-heritage/transformingsociety/livinglearning/coll-9-health1/health-06/ . Also . https://www.parliament.uk/vagabondact.

[37] See http://www.workhouses.org.uk/poorlaws/1601act.shtml.

Overseers were required to be appointed and were to be responsible for collecting the tax and paying it to those in need in accordance with the law. The Justices of the Peace also had enforcement power and they presumably could resort to bailiffs if necessary, but this seems to have been a rare occurrence. Given that everyone (and that means everyone) attended regularly at church services, this would have made the collection of such taxes that much easier. In such a case, those that owed money came to you rather than the other way around. Also, failure to pay might well have been quite a public affair.

It has not been possible to determine precisely how the amount of money due from each person was calculated. The Overseers had the power to levy the rates and they presumably could work out the basis on which they should be paid. The rate was calculated on a rateable value or 'rate-in-the-pound' basis, so each property must have had such a value assigned to it. It is certainly the case that there would have been much discussion around this but evidence has not been found of any disputes nor any records of the rateable values themselves, although aggrieved ratepayers could get relief at quarter-sessions.[38] The rateable values would, as today, have been carried forward from one year to the next and used by the Overseers to calculate what was due. The values would have been subject to amendment where, for instance, a holding was divided, and new occupants and/or owners would have taken over all or part of a holding from time to time. All of this suggests that a separate record must have been kept of the local properties subject to the tax. However, no such record has so far been found.

From the Widecombe Overseers' Accounts it certainly appears as if the tax is levied on property rather than on individuals per se. All amounts state a person (or 'occupier') and a holding. There are no Accounts that just list individual persons.

In general, no doubt, Widecombe was a relatively wealthy place, given the presence of tin mining and farming, even if there was a huge divide, as always seems to be the case, between those who had and those who had not. There would have been exceptions, of course, but those that genuinely could not pay their dues would probably have left their occupation of those premises liable to the tax, or borrowed money to see them through bad times.

---

[38] Church, 'The Compleat Parish Officer' - page 61.

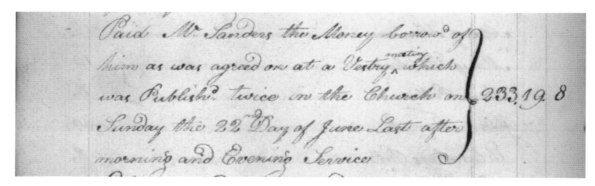

FIGURE 7-3: DETAIL FROM THE OVERSEERS' ACCOUNT BOOK FROM 1818 SHOWING THE REPAYMENT OF A LOAN FROM MR SANDERS

(IMAGE A007.008.P036 FROM THE WIDECOMBE ARCHIVE)

The years 1818/1819 provide an interesting example of the flexibility that could be applied to the collection of the Poor Rate, and reflect the often repeated clause 'to be collected as often as necessary'. In April 1818 there is a Poor Rate collected at ninepence in the pound. Then in June 1818 and February 1819 there are two further rates collected at four shillings and sixpence in the pound (each being six times as much as the April 1818 rate). This meant that substantial sums were raised in that year. The reasons are not hard to establish. Firstly, the amounts paid out had increased (although not massively), and, secondly, in January 1818 there was a repayment to a Mr Sanders of a loan of £233 19s 8d (see Figure 7-3). Interestingly, no previous reference to this loan either in terms of capital amounts paid over or interest payments made has been found.[39]

The transcript of Figure 7-3 is as follows:

Paid Mr Sanders the Money borrow[d] of
him as was agreed on at a Vestry meeting which
was Publish[d] twice in the Church on
Sunday the 22nd Day of June Last after
morning and Evening Service

This also shows quite clearly the method of publicising decisions: announcements were twice made at Church Services.

That the underlying accounts were undoubtedly much more complicated than shown is evidenced by what went on in 1815. There were considerable arrears listed going back to 1809 with no evidence of successful collection. There were also two repayments to Mr Tozer of seventy pounds, presumably reflecting another loan. (See A007.005.p029 - A007.005.p031 in the Widecombe Archive). Clearly, much closer

---

[39] Generally, in this period of the French wars and afterwards, rents and prices appear to have increased substantially and perhaps this had something to do with increases in the poor rate - see Evans 1976 The Contentious Tithe pages 30-31. measuringworth.com shows that the retail price index in 1793 was 1.093 and by 1813 had peaked at 1.965 before falling back again to 1.69 by 1819.

examination of these accounts could be carried out, if only to understand how they balanced and reconciled! Dedicated volunteers always welcome!!

SPENDING THE POOR RATE

There is a wealth of information in the Overseers' Accounts regarding payments of money to those in need as well as all the other expenses of administering the poor relief system. Some of these wider aspects (such as Apprenticeships and Removal Orders) are dealt with in later chapters. To provide some examples of direct payments to the poor, the specific year of 1804-5 is examined in some detail below with a full transcript of the year accessible via Appendix A. Examination of these records shows the wide range of matters that had to be dealt with at times, from rushing to fetch a doctor, to dealing with errant parishioners who wandered into neighbouring parishes, and also to burying the dead.

During the year, the accounts record thirteen months of payments of various kinds, many regular payments to those in need (which suggest they were made four-weekly). They were also special payments on Good Friday and Easter Monday, effectively rounding off payments for the year.[40] Figure 7-4 below shows the payments for Good Friday and Figure 7-5 shows the remaining payments for Good Friday together with those made on Easter Monday.

There were 35 payments made on Good Friday plus a further 12 payments to various recipients re 'BC' (this is an abbreviation for 'Bastard' or 'Base' Child).

These payments were generally classified as 'pay' which might suggest that the recipients did work for which they received payment, but this is not particularly clear. There may well be a mixture of those who can do some work and those who cannot. How this was organised in Widecombe (if it was) is unclear. It is possible that the able poor helped out if they could at busy times, e.g. at harvest time. The first (very regular) monthly entries in the accounts are likely to be pension payments, i.e. payments to the elderly or infirm, of course long before the days of any retirement pension or state aid. We can deduce this both from the regular nature of the payments and specifically from 1804-1805 where expenses are recorded for the burial of a number of those who previously received such regular payments, and although this might be a coincidence, it seems likely that they died at least partly as a result of their age. By 'pension' we should note that it does not necessarily equate to 'elderly'. Those who were incapacitated will also have received such regular

---

[40] It is difficult to precisely establish the basis for payment. If there were four-weekly payments then thirteen months would equate to 52 weeks and there would be no need for an additional two-week payment. On the other hand, the 1803-1804 accounts start in the 'second month' and end in the twelfth and the Good Friday payments are for three weeks. See Appendix A for full details.

	£	s	d
Good Fridays Pay			
Isaac Brooking	0	7	0
Rebecca Brook	0	6 +	
Wm. French	0	8	
Margery Ford	0	6	
Mary Leaman Dunstone	0	4 +	
Sarah Hannaford	0	4	
Richd. Leaman	0	5	6
Elizt. Leaman	0	4	
Mary Stancombe	0	5 +	
Wm. Stancombe	0	4	
Mary Smerdon	0	3	6..
Joan White	0	5	
John Townsend	0	4	
Ann Winddat	0	3 + 6	
Joan French	0	3	
Sarah Baker	0	2	
Jane Middletons children	0	8	
Charity Lee	0	1	6..
John Warren	0	6 +	
Susanna Smerdon	0	4	
Ann Hamlyn	0	4 +	
Epaphany Griffen	0	4	
Sarah Hamlyn	0	2	6
Roger Townsend	0	5	
Mary Brooking	0	2 +	
Elizb. Children	0	6	6..
John Norrish	0	4	
Mary Caunter	0	2	
Richard Crispin	0	4	
Richard Stancombe	0	4 +	
Wm. Leaman	0	3	
Mary Leaman Bimph	0	4	
Susanna Lawrence	0	4	
Mary Stanbury 7-2 pay	3	15 +	
Johnna Murch 1-2 pay	0	12	
Elizb. Potter BC	0	3 + 6	
Mary Coakers BC	0	2	
Jane Coakers BC	0	2	
Elizt. Leaman BC	0	2	
Ann Leaman and her BC	0	5	
Ann Turners BC one weeks pay	0	1	3..
Ann Pikes BC	0	3	
Grace Thorne BC	0	2	
Ann Leamans BC Town	0	2 +	
Elizt. Withycombes BC	0	3	6
Margery anchantons BC	0	3	
Pd. 52 Weeks pay for Peter Willcocks Substitutes Family at 3s per Week	7	16 +	
pd. 13-2 pay to Ann Hamlyn BC at 7-3 for 1805	3	7	6..
pd. James Baster with his Apprentice	0	14 +	
pd. for Instructions left last year apprentice	0	3	
pd. for a Hat for Farmer Barters	0	2	6
Ditto Farmer French Royal signal	2	2	6..
Usual expence	0	8	6
pd. a County rate and Half	4	0	5½
	29	7	8¼

FIGURE 7-4: DETAIL FROM THE OVERSEERS' ACCOUNT BOOK FROM 1805 SHOWING MONEY PAYMENTS (IMAGE A006.006.P021 FROM THE WIDECOMBE ARCHIVE)

46

payments. The accounts do not indicate the details of why the payment was being made.[41] This is most likely because those who agreed the accounts or inspected them (such as the ratepayers who might want to know how their money was being spent) would have been local people and would have known who the people were and their circumstances.[42]

The amounts paid on Good Friday 1805 vary from 2s up to approximately 8s with no real indication of why, although it may be to do with dependants or whether they are 'in' poor (i.e. residing in the poor house) or 'out' poor (i.e. residing elsewhere). For instance, *'Ann Pikes BC'* gets 3s whereas *'Grace Thorns BC'* gets 2s. As mentioned above, these Good Friday payments were one half of the normal payments to these individuals. This was because they were payments for two weeks only, whereas the normal payment was a monthly one.

One fascinating entry shows a payment of £7 16s *"pd 52 Weeks pay for Peter Willcocks Substitutes Family at 3s per Week"*. This is about the same time as entries recording the payment of bounty for residents in connection with the Militia and so this is most likely to be a payment to the family of someone who agreed to act as a substitute i.e. to join the Militia in his stead). Another possibility (that seems less likely) is that this is a form of adoption or foster-care where Peter Willcocks has no relations of his own and is residing with another family which is being paid 3 shillings per week to look after him.

Then (see Figure 7-5), there are further payments to people *'in need'* and quite a high payment of £1 6s 2½d to Wm Smerdon *"with an apprentice"*. Perhaps William Smerdon could not afford to look after the apprentice without help, or this was a form of premium payment to induce him to take an apprentice on. For more information about apprenticeships, see Chapter 8 on The Apprenticeship System.

On Easter Monday various other payments were made of which the highlights are as follows:

---

[41] Except for the use of 'BC' to indicate a base or bastard child as is discussed elsewhere.

[42] See Oxley, 1974 (page 54), who highlights cases where the first item in the Overseers' Accounts was the pension list and this was followed by the miscellaneous expenditure: exactly the situation we find in the Widecombe Accounts.

CLOTHING

There are various entries concerning the provision of clothing. Clothing was clearly arranged collectively and in addition to payments of money. The payment for the making of shoes is especially significant:

for making pair Breeches fo Wm Stancombe 1s 2d

for making Waiscoat for John Warren 1s

for making Coat for Richd Crispin and Canvas for ye same 2s

p^d Wm Cleaves Bill for Shoes for the poor people £10 15s 11d

GENERAL OUTGOINGS

There are a whole host of general outgoings of one sort or another that arise at various times. Just from this Easter Monday account we see:

"*pd for Delivering Margaret White 3s 6d*" (Presumably of her baby - it is to be noted also that Margaret White is paid 6s each month during this period).

"*pd for Paper and Candles 1s 6d*" (presumably for use in the poor house)

"*for Blanket for Mary Stancombe 7s 6d*" (perhaps for cover whilst sleeping)

"*pd for Writing this Acct 7s*" (it does not say to whom this payment is made - perhaps the clerk, although he is paid a salary)

"*pd the Doctors Bill £10 13s 10d*" (Annual retainer for being available to look after the health of the poor - see 'Medical Help' below for more details)

"*pd the Doctor for John Wreyford 13s*" (This must have been outside the terms of the retainer)

"*pd ye Constable for returning a Summons Concerning Elizb Withycombe 3s 6d*" (people clearly got into the odd bit of bother from time to time)

"*pd for Bringing home John Hamlyn Goods 4s 6d*"

	£	s	d
for 3 Gounds for Wm. Rubys Children	0	7	6
pd. Wm. Smerdon with an apprentice	1	6	2½
Margaret White	0	7	6
Grace French in Need	0	2	
Ditto 2 Journeys to Doctor	0	1	6
Rachel Hannaford in Need	0	3	6
Elizb. Turner in Need	0	5	
Jane Warren in Need	0	2	
Margery Ford in Need	0	1	
Ann Potter in Need	0	1	
Edward Smerdon 2-2 pay	1	0	
	3	17	2½
	29	7	8¼
pd. in all on Good Friday	33	4	10¾

pd. on Easter Monday

	£	s	d
for making pair Breeches for Wm. Stancombe	0	1	2
for making Waiscoat for John Warren	0	1	
pd. Wm. Norrish Butcher with an apprentice	1	6	2½
for making Coat for Richd. Crispin and Canvas for ye same	0	2	
pd. Wm. Cleaves Bill for Shoes for the poor people	10	15	11
pd. Wm. Beards Bill	3	1	
pd. for Delivering Margaret White	0	3	6
pd. for Paper and Candles	0	1	6
for Blanket for Mary Stancombe	0	7	6
pd. for Writing this Acct	0	7	
pd. for Postage of a Letter sent by the Justice of ye peace	0	0	4½
pd. the Doctors Bill	10	13	10
pd. the Doctor for John Wreyford	0	13	
pd. Mr. Jerves's Bill	1	6	6
pd. ye Constable for Warning a Summons concerning Elizb. Withycombe		3	6
pd. for bringing home John Hamlyns Goods	0	4	6
pd. for postage of a Letter concerning Sarah Dodges	0	0	4½
	29	8	10½
Elizb. Leaman in Need	0	3	
	29	11	10½

FIGURE 7-5: DETAIL FROM THE OVERSEERS' ACCOUNT BOOK FROM 1805 SHOWING MONEY PAYMENTS
(IMAGE A006.006.P022 FROM THE WIDECOMBE ARCHIVE)

Also in the accounts for that year is the following:

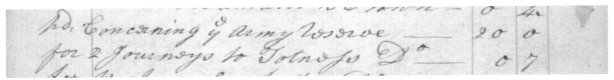

This reads: *"pd concerning ye Army Reserve [£]20 0[s]'* (this was probably to do with the British anti-invasion preparations of 1803–05, being the military and civilian responses to Napoleon's planned invasion of the United Kingdom.) There is also the second line which is connected: *"for 2 journeys to Totnes Do [£]0 7[s]'*, where "Do" means "Ditto" suggesting the journeys were in connection with the Army Reserve.

The Overseers also seem to have been responsible for paying the 'County Rate'. See, for instance A006.005.p012 where '*3 County Rates and a half'* are paid totalling £9 7s 8¼d. From this it can be concluded that at this time (and in fact up until much more recently) the collection of the Poor Rate included an amount for the County Rate.

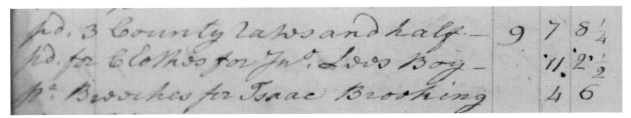

It was hard to resist transcribing the other two lines in Figure 7-7:

pd. for Clothes for Jnº Lees Boy 11[s] 2½[d]
pʳ. Breeches for Isaac Brooking 4[s] 6[d]

The full transcript of the accounts for the 1804-1805 year is available via Appendix A.

NEGOTIATION

There was even an element of negotiation evidenced in the select vestry minutes of 30ᵗʰ November 1821, where Ann Tremills had applied for maintenance for her child.

A transcript of the above is as follows:

Ann Tremills
who applied for a weekly allowance for the
Maintenance of her child 1s/6d a week was
offered to her which being refused 1s/9d was
proposed - and that sum was also refused
2s/ being the sum which she demanded

This negotiation does not appear to have been resolved at the meeting.

THE POORHOUSE OR WORKHOUSE

FIGURE 7-9: THE WESTERN END OF THE CHURCH HOUSE AS IT IS TODAY

(IMAGE COPYRIGHT THE AUTHOR)

FIGURE 7-10: EARLY PHOTOGRAPH OF THE CHURCH HOUSE WHEN THATCHED, WITH ST. PANCRAS CHURCH TOWER IN THE BACKGROUND

(IMAGE H380.002 FROM THE WIDECOMBE ARCHIVE)

ESTABLISHMENT OF THE WIDECOMBE WORKHOUSE

As far as we know, the poorhouse or workhouse in Widecombe has always been situated in the Church House. This is the most, if not the only, substantial building in Widecombe that was in existence and in parish ownership and therefore it was the obvious place to locate this public welfare provision. Today, the Church House is in the care of the National Trust.

From the information that we have it looks as if the use of the Church House as a poor house or workhouse was usually shared with other uses. Thus we know that rooms in the Church House were rented out for the purposes of 'schooling' in 1804 (see the chapter on The Church Rate above). It is likely that the upstairs was used for schooling while the downstairs was used as a poor house.

It is hard to be certain when these uses started. If we look at the Episcopal Visitation Return of 1744[43] we see that there was no 'publick' or Charity School at that time, but there was an alms-house, which we can perhaps reasonably assume is the Church House.

Even today the ground floor of the Church House is cold, damp and draughty on a winter's day. It can certainly be bleak at times up on the moor. Perhaps a roaring fire helped (if there was one), but one can imagine conditions not being particularly enjoyable.

IMPROVING THE WORKHOUSE

There was an agreement to improve the workhouse ('fit it out' etc.) in Widecombe in 1814. This is shown in Figure 7-11 and note that although this states '*setting up*' this probably just means 'according to the new rules' as the text of the document includes the words '*our present Workhouse*', suggesting that the Workhouse was already in use.

This agreement stated that the Parish of Widecombe would comply with the requirements of the 'Act for the Better Relief and Employment of the Poor' (22nd George the Third c 83[44]), even though this Act became law in 1782 (i.e. 32 years earlier!)

In order to provide these sorts of facilities the workhouse (the Church House in Widecombe's case) needed to be upgraded. The agreement also provided for the appointment of governesses as paid positions.

---

[43] See Appendix C.

[44] see Webb 1927 page 272 - this was known as Gilbert's Act after Thomas Gilbert, M.P. for Lichfield who had been pressing for years for Poor Law reform.

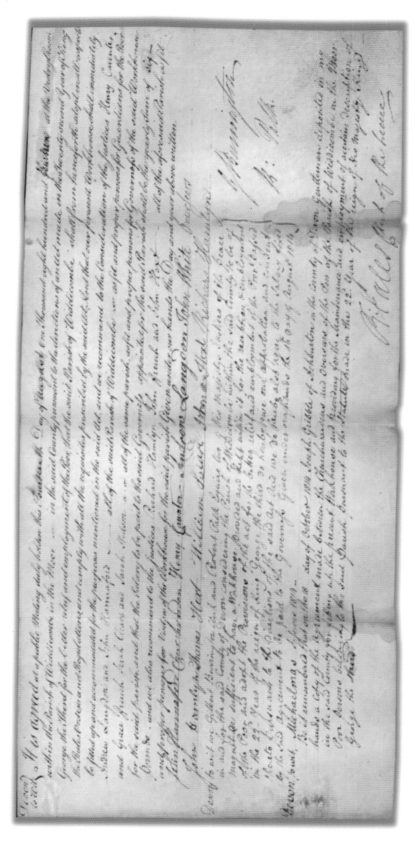

FIGURE 7-11: AGREEMENT MADE AT A PUBLIC MEETING RELATING TO THE POOR ACT AND SETTING UP THE IMPROVED WORKHOUSE IN WIDDICOMBE

(IMAGE A025.005 FROM THE WIDECOMBE ARCHIVE)

Devon to wit
It is agreed at a public Meeting duly holden this fourteenth Day of August one
Thousand eight hundred and fourteen at the Vestry Room
within the Parish of Widdicombe in the Moor - in the said County pursuant to the
directions of an Act made in the Twenty second Year of King
George the Third for the better relief and employment of the Poor, that the said
Parish of Widdicombe shall from henceforth adopt in all aspects
the Rules Orders and Regulations and comply with all the requisites prescribed by
the said Act And that our present Workhouse shall immediately
be fitted up and accommodated for the purposes mentioned in the said Act, and we
recommend to the Consideration of the Justices Henry Caunter
Andrew Langdon and John Hannaford all of the said Parish of Widdicombe all as fit
and proper persons for Guardians for the Poor
and Grace Ffrench Sarah Cleave and Sarah Stidson - - all of the same parish as fit and
proper persons for Governess of the said Workhouse
for the said parish and that the Salary to be paid to the said Governess appointed for
the said Parish shall be the yearly Sum of six-
Pounds. and we also recommend to the Justices Richard Hamlyn John Ffrench and
John Hext all of the aforesaid Parish as fit
and proper persons for Visitors of the Workhouse for the said parish Given under
our hands that Day and year above written
John Hannaford Churchwarden Henry Caunter Andrew Langdon John White
Overseers
John Hamlyn Thomas Hext William Seiard [or Seward?] John Hext Richard Hamlyn

Devon
to wit we Gilbert Burrington Clerk and Robert Palk Esquire two of His Majestys
Justices of the Peace
in and for the said County of Devon considering the Parish of Widdicombe within
the said County to be of
magnitude sufficient to have a Workhouse provided and kept within it for the
reception & employment
of the Poor and adopt the Provisions of the act for the better relief and employment
of the Poor passed
in the 22d Year of the reign of King George the third do hereby give our approbation
and consent
thereto pursuant to the directions of the said Act And we do hereby also agree to the
Salary fixed
by the said Agreement to be paid to the Governess Given under our hands the 10th
day of August 1814
G Burrington
R: Palk
Devon to wit
Michaelmas Sessions 1814 -

(continued overleaf…)

(…continued from previous page)

Be it remembered that on the 18 day of October 1814 Joseph Gribble of Ashburton in the County of Devon Gentleman deposited in my
hands a Copy of the Agreement made between the Churchwardens and Overseers of the Poor of the Parish of Widdicombe in the Moor
in the said County for fitting up the present Workhouse and providing for the Maintenance and employment of a certain description of
Poor persons belonging to the said parish pursuant to the Statute made in the 22d Year of the reign if His Majesty King
George the third
R Eales Clerk of the peace

Note that in A023.p031 there is a note that £8 5s 7d was paid to Mr Gribble for 'Licensing Workhouse', which suggests that the work identified above has been carried out.

The document confirming Grace French as governess of the poor is also in the archive (Figure 7-12):

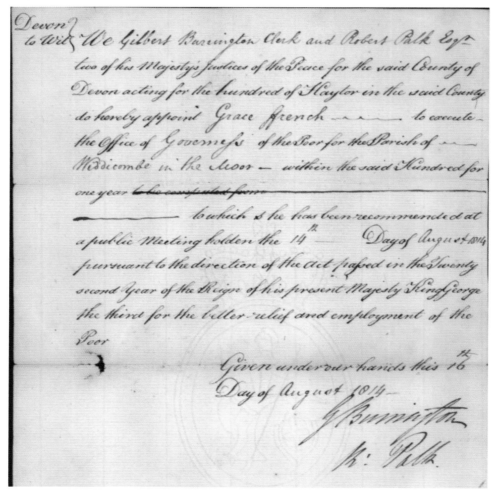

FIGURE 7-12: DOCUMENT APPOINTING GRACE FRENCH AS GOVERNESS OF THE POOR IN 1814
(IMAGE A052A.601 FROM THE WIDECOMBE ARCHIVE)

Devon to Wit
We Gilbert Barrington Clerk and Robert Palk Esqr
two of his Majesty's Justices of the Peace for the said County of
Devon acting for the hundred of Haytor in the said County
do hereby appoint Grace ffrench to execute
the Office of Governess of the Poor for the Parish of
Widdicombe in the Moor - within the said Hundred for
one year
to which she has been recommended at
a public Meeting holden the 14th Day of August 1814
pursuant to the direction of the Act passed in the Twenty
second year of the Reign of his present Majesty King George
the third for the better relief and employment of the
Poor
Given under our hands this 16th
Day of August 1814
G Burrington
R: Palk

INTERESTING ASIDE 2: STAMP DUTY

Stamp Duty has been levied in various forms on paper instruments and other items since 1694, with many subsequent changes, either as embossed stamps or as postage stamps. Examples in the text are the 2d (two pence) postage stamp on the Poor Rate Receipt of 1921 (Figure 10-12), the 3s 6d 'stamped' stamp on the 1814 indenture relating to the Widecombe Education Charity (Figure 11-1) and those on the various apprenticeship indentures: see for example the 2d stamp on the 1735 indenture of Katherine Courters(Figure 8-8).

2d stamps on receipts were required by law for payments of £2 and upwards (The Stamp Act 1891), and so we see that the Special Expenses Receipt for 4s 4d (Figure 10-13) had no stamp. This duty was abolished in 1964.

DIET

We get a glimpse into the food allowances in the poorhouse of Widecombe from a sheet that was found amongst the apprenticeship records in the parish chest (see Figure 7-13).

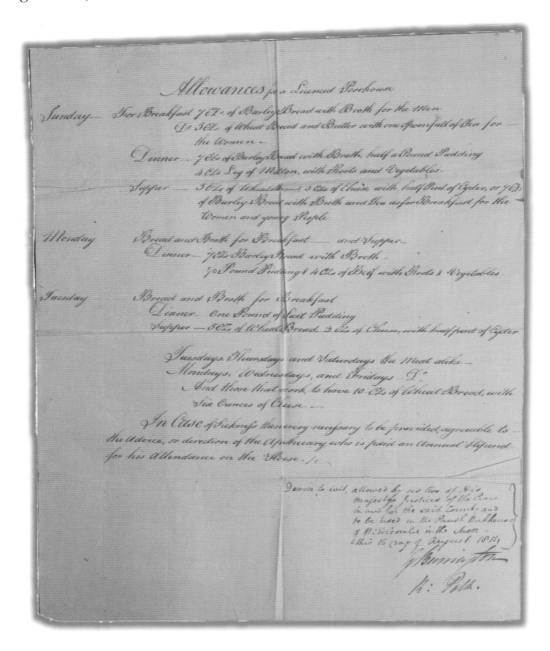

FIGURE 7-13: DOCUMENT SHOWING THE FOOD ALLOWANCES FOR A LICENCED POORHOUSE IN 1814

(IMAGE A052A.611.F FROM THE WIDECOMBE ARCHIVE)

The transcription of this allowance is shown below and it is clear that, in Widecombe at least, these provisions are to be followed.

Allowances for a Licenced Poorhouse
Sunday For Breakfast 7 OZs of Barley Bread with Broth for the Men
Do 5 OZs of Wheat Bread and Butter with one Spoonfull of Tea for
The Women ~
Dinner 7 OZs of Barley Bread with Broth half a Pound Pudding
4 OZs Leg of Mutton, with Roots and Vegetables
Supper 5 OZs of Wheat Bread 3 OZs of Cheese with half Pint of Cyder or 7 OZs
Of Barley Bread with Broth and Tea as for Breakfast for the
Women and young People
Monday Bread and Broth for Breakfast and Supper
Dinner – 7 OZs Barley Bread with Broth
½ Pound Pudding & 4 OZs of Beef with Roots
Tuesday Bread and Broth for Breakfast
Dinner One Pound of Suet Pudding
Supper – 5 OZs of Wheat Bread 3 OZs of Cheese with half pint of Cyder
Tuesdays Thursdays and Saturdays the Meal alike –
Mondays, Wednesdays, and Fridays Do
And those that work, to have 10 OZs of Wheat Bread, with
Six Ounces of Cheese.-
In Case of Sickness then every necessary to be provided agreeable to
The advice, or direction of the Apothecary, who is paid an Annual Stipend
For his Attendance on the House./-
Devon to wit, allowed by us two of his
Majestys Justices of the Peace
In and for the said County and
To be used in the Parish Workhouse
Of Widdicombe in the Moor
This 16 day of August 1814
J Burrington
R: Palk

All in all, this appears to be a reasonably good diet, albeit a bit repetitive and limited in scope. It would be interesting to compare the diet of parishioners who were outside the poor system and had to fend for themselves!

LATER RELATIONSHIP WITH THE NEWTON ABBOT UNION WORKHOUSE

The Church House continued to be used as a workhouse for some time after the Newton Abbot Union was formed (see Chapter 10). A flavour of the relationship between the two, and of the status and ownership of the Church House, is given by these notes in the Select Vestry Minutes Book (Figure 7-14 and Figure 7-15), which adequately expresses, it is felt, the independent nature of the Widecombe contingent. The presumption is that these were notes intended to act as a record of the actual letter sent.

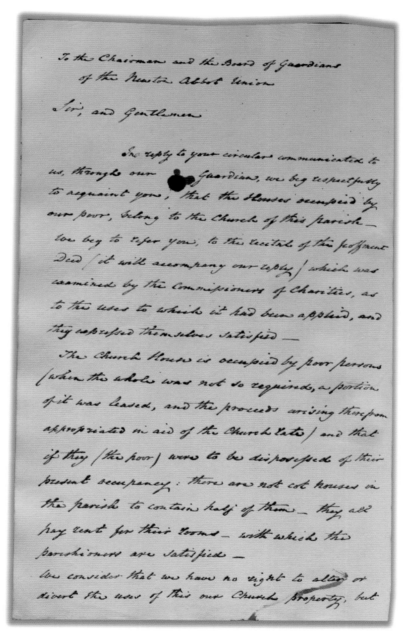

FIGURE 7-14: EXTRACT FROM THE SELECT VESTRY MINUTE BOOK (UNDATED)
SEE ALSO FIGURE 7-15 (DOCUMENT 2955A/PV/1 FROM THE SW HERITAGE TRUST DEVON ARCHIVES)

The transcription of the record shown in Figure 7-14 and Figure 7-15 is shown below.

To the Chairman and the Board of Guardians
of the Newton Abbot Union
Sir, and Gentlemen
In reply to your circular communicated to
us, through our Guardian, we beg respectfully
to acquaint you, that the Houses occupied by
our poor, belong to the Church of this Parish
We beg to refer you, to the recitals of the feoffment
Deed (it will accompany our reply) which was
examined by the Commissioners of Charities, as
to the uses to which it had been applied, and
they expressed themselves satisfied
The Church House is occupied by poor persons
(when the whole was not so required, a portion
of it was leased, and the proceeds arising therefrom
appropriated in aid of the Church later) and that
if they (the poor) were to be dispossessed of their
present occupancy : there are not cot houses in
the Parish to contain half of them - they all
pay rent for their rooms - with which the
Parishioners are satisfied-
We consider that we have no right to alter or
divert the uses of this our Church property, but

(Second page Figure 7-15)

on the contrary to resist any attempt to effect it
and not an Individual who attends this meeting has
expressed any other wish
We are ready & willing to rate this property with
all other property in the Parish, and to pay from
the rents received such Sums as shall from time
to time become due as Poor Rates - and further
it is our wish to do this with as little delay as
possible - the alteration in the rating we understand
is to take place from Lady day next
Present
JH Mason Vicar
John Easterbrook Churchwarden
John Hannaford John Townsend
Daniel Hext Jno Langdon
Richard Hamlyn Joseph Leaman
Nicholas Easterbrook William Stidston
John French James Hamlyn
Roger Hannaford

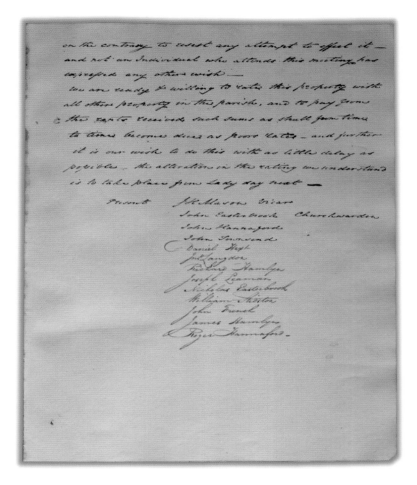

FIGURE 7-15: SECOND PAGE OF THE EXTRACT FROM THE SELECT VESTRY MINUTE BOOK (UNDATED)

SEE ALSO FIGURE 7-14 (DOCUMENT 2955A/PV/1 FROM THE SW HERITAGE TRUST DEVON ARCHIVES)

It would be interesting to follow this correspondence through but nothing further on this subject has been found in the Widecombe records so far.

MEDICAL HELP

Full medical help was provided to recipients of poor relief. The Overseers' Accounts are peppered with costs for attendance for various ailments, plus of course childbirth.

In the parish records is an agreement from 1824 with the physician R.P. Mogridge to attend the poor for the succeeding twelve months at a fixed cost of nine guineas (£9 9s). See Figure 7-16.

An interesting example of the treatment provided by Mr Mogridge is indicated by the account of the medicines supplied in 1819 (see Figure 7-17). It also shows how often he made a journey to Widecombe - almost daily at times (although it is also noted that the retainer discussed above clearly did not include travel costs as these are claimed separately).

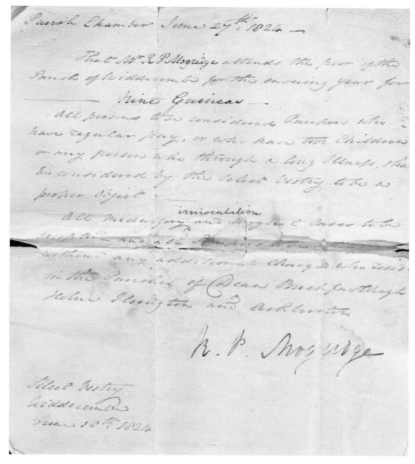

FIGURE 7-16: DOCUMENT SHOWING AN AGREEMENT FROM 1824 WITH THE PHYSICIAN R.P. MOGRIDGE TO ATTEND THE POOR FOR THE NEXT TWELVE MONTHS

(IMAGE A025.002 FROM THE WIDECOMBE ARCHIVE)

The transcription of the agreement in Figure 7-16 is as follows:

Parish Chamber June 27: 1824
That Mr R P Mogridge attends the poor of the Parish of Widdicombe for the ensuing
year for
Nine Guineas
All persons to be considered Paupers who have regular pay[*], or who know two
Children or any persons who through a long illness, tha[t] is considered by the select
Vestry to be a proper Object
All Midwifery innoculation and surgical cases to be excepted - and all Paupers to be
attended without any additional charges who resid[e] in the Parishes of Dean
Buckfastleigh Holne Ilsington and Ashburton
R. P. Mogridge
Select Vestry
Widdecombe
Juan 18th 1824

* 'pay' here must relate to paupers who have regular pay from the Poor Rate rather than our modern-day usage of pay from employment.

FIGURE 7-17: DOCUMENT SHOWING THE MEDICINES SUPPLIED IN 1819 BY THE PHYSICIAN J. MOGRIDGE
WHILST ATTENDING THE POOR

(IMAGE A052.394 FROM THE WIDECOMBE ARCHIVE)

1819	Widecombe Parish to J Mogridge			
Aug 26	John Brooking's Wife a Journey		5	
	a Cordial Mixture		2	6
	a Purging Mixture		2	6
	a Sudorific Mixture		2	6
27	the Purging Mixture		2	6
28	a Journey		5	
	the Cordial Mixture		2	6
	the Sudorific Mixture		2	6
	Cordial Drops		1	
29	a Journey		5	
	the Purging Mixture		2	6
	the Sudorific Mixture		2	6
30	Do		2	6
	the Cordial Mixture		2	6
	a Journey		5	
31	Do		5	
Sep 1	Do		5	
	the Cordial Mixture		2	6
	the Sudorific Mixture		2	6
	a Journey		5	
3	an Anodyne Mixture		2	6
	the Cordial Mixture		2	6
6	a Journey		5	
8	Do		5	
	the Anodyne Mixture		2	6
	the Cordial Mixture		2	6
11	Do		2	6
	the Anodyne Mixture		2	6
	a Journey		5	
16	Do		5	
	the Cordial Mixture		2	6
25	[Do]		2	6
	the Purging Mixture		2	6
Oct 2	the Cordial Mixture		2	6
13	Do		2	6
16	Tincture for the Tooth Ache		1	
Nov 2	the Purging Mixture		2	6
	[the Cordial Mixture]		[2]	[6]
			—	—
		6	9	6
		—	—	—

The addition does not appear to add up properly, but perhaps there are other items not preserved.

FIGURE 7-18: THOMAS ROWLANDSON (1757-1827): COUNTRY CHARACTERS - DOCTOR. 1799

(THE ELISHA WHITTELSEY COLLECTION, METROPOLITAN MUSEUM OF ART, PUBLIC DOMAIN)

FOXES

Provision was included in the Overseers' Accounts for paying for the capture and killing of foxes and other 'vermin'. That this was necessary indicates perhaps that there were many more foxes around than is experienced on the moor today (it would appear generally that there was much more wildlife around than we find today - most of it eradicated since by a combination of 'sport', hunting, farming and other practices). The unpleasant and gruesome task of controlling the fox population was down to individuals, although quite why it all falls under the remit of the Poor Rate is difficult to understand.

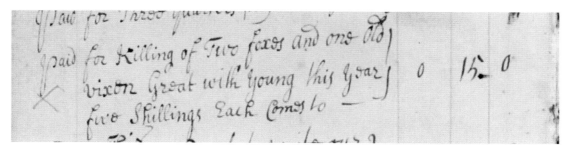

FIGURE 7-19: DETAIL FROM THE OVERSEERS' ACCOUNTS FOR 1804 SHOWING PAYMENT MADE FOR KILLING FOXES

(IMAGE A003.P008 FROM THE WIDECOMBE ARCHIVE)

Figure 7-19 provides an example of a payment for killing foxes. The transcript is as follows:

paid for Killing of Two foxes and one Old vixen Great with young this year five shillings Each Comes to 15s

There is an interesting aside of a dispute arising over this process (see Figure 7-20).

In 1761 there was an incident in which some farmers went out to kill some foxes and accidentally killed a hare. Someone reported them and they were fined £5 - a lot of money. It turned out that the person who reported them was someone the parish employed to catch foxes and he was paid well by the parish for each one he brought in. Figure 7-20 below records the meeting at which the signatories unanimously agreed to make him catch sufficient foxes to make up for the fine before they would resume paying him.

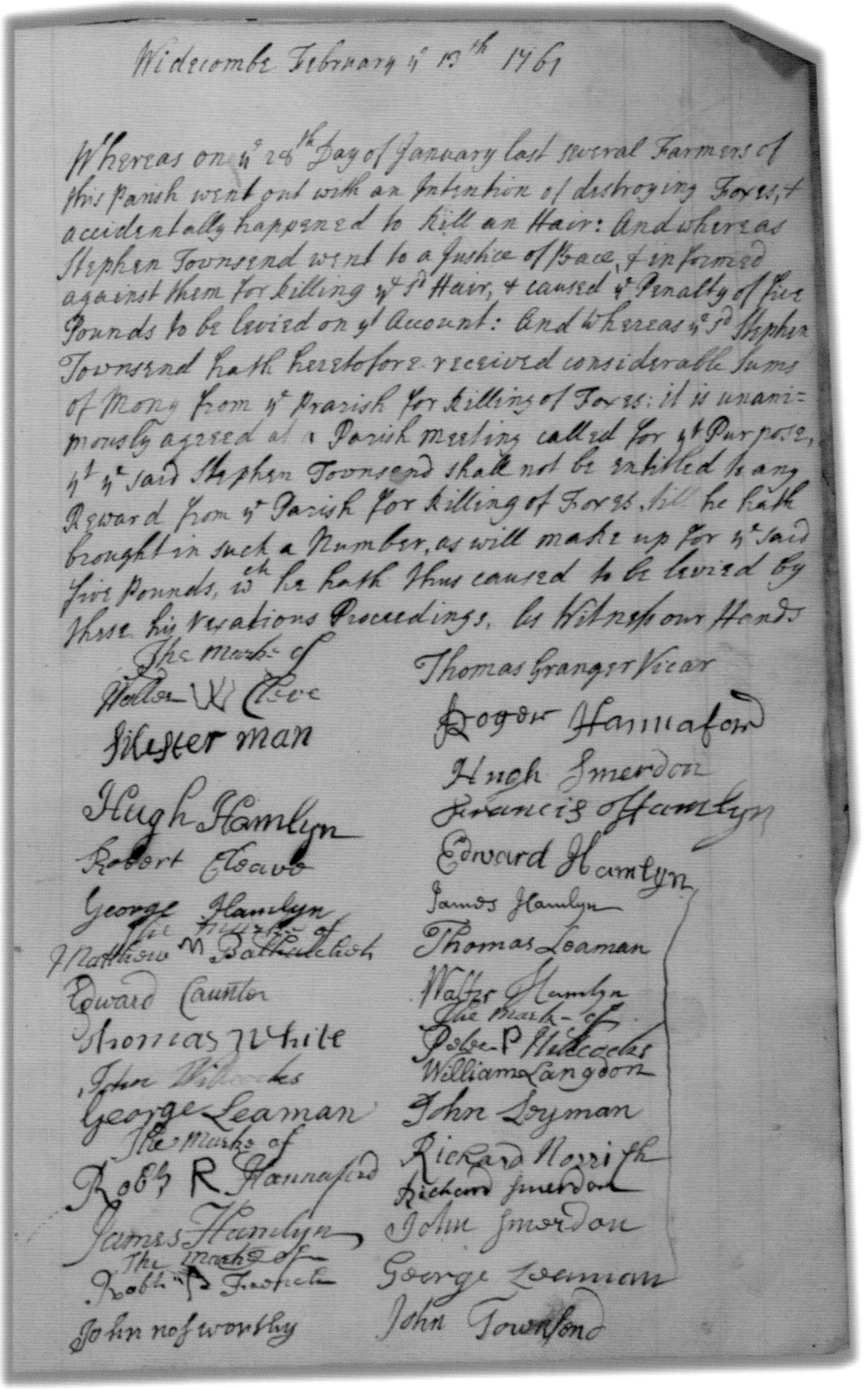

FIGURE 7-20: DETAIL FROM THE OVERSEERS' ACCOUNTS FOR 1761 SHOWING THE COMPLAINT ABOUT KILLING FOXES

(IMAGE A004.P225 FROM THE WIDECOMBE ARCHIVE)

The transcript of Figure 7-20 is as follows:

Widecombe February ye 13th 1761
Whereas on yᵉ 28ᵗʰ Day of January last several Farmers of
this Parish went out with an Intention of destroying Foxes &
accidentally happened to kill an Hair: And whereas
Stephen Townsend went to a Justice of Peace & informed
against them for killing yᵉ sᵈ Hair, & caused yᵉ Penalty of five
Pounds to be levied on yᵉ Account: and whereas yᵉ sᵈ Stephen
Townsend hath heretofore received considerable sums
of Money from yᵉ Parish for killing of Foxes: it is unani-
mously agreed at a Parish meeting called for yᵉ Purpose,
[That] yᵉ said Stephen Townsend shall not be entitled to any
Reward from yᵉ Parish for killing of Foxes till he hath
brought in such a Number, as will make up for yᵉ said
five pounds wᶜʰ he hath thus caused to be levied by
these his vexatious Proceedings, be Witness our Hands

the mark of	*Thomas Granger Vicar*
Haller W Cleve	
Silester man	*Roger Hannaford*
	Hugh Smerdon
Hugh Hamlyn	*Francis Hamlyn*
Robert Cleave	*Edward Hamlyn*
George Hamlyn	*James Hamlyn*
The mark of	
Matthew M Bathulcheh	*Thomas Leaman*
Edward Caunter	*Walter Hamlyn*
	The Mark of
Thomas White	*Peter P Wilcocks*
John Willcocks	*William Langdon*
George Leaman	*John Leyman*
The Marke of	
Robt R Hannaford	*Richard Norrish*
	Richard Smerdon
James Hamlyn	*John Smerdon*
the Marke of	
Robt R French	*George Leaman*
John Nosworthy	*John Townsend*

DEALING WITH THE DEAD

The Widecombe Overseers' Accounts for account years 1734/5-1735/6 provide some interesting entries relating to the necessary dealing with the dead. See especially Figure 7-21 and Figure 7-22 below, both from archive reference A003.p008. The entries relate to Thomas Greep, who was found dead on the Moor, and also to the practice of burying the dead in a woollen shroud. The Overseers also had to deal with any deaths of the poor in their care.

THOMAS GREEP

Thomas Greep was found dead on the moor sometime between 1734 and 1736 and his body had to be dealt with by the parish. Figure 7-21 shows the entry in the Overseers' Accounts:

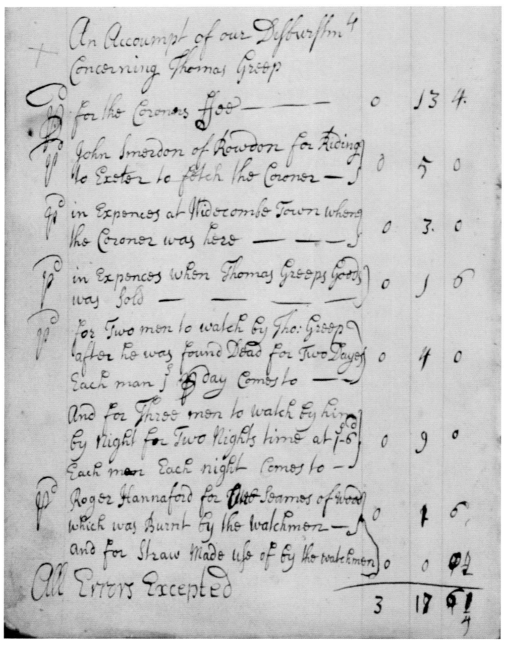

FIGURE 7-21: DETAIL FROM THE OVERSEERS' ACCOUNTS FOR 1734/5 CONCERNING THE DEALING WITH THE DEATH OF THOMAS GREEP FOUND DEAD ON THE MOOR

(IMAGE A003.P008 FROM THE WIDECOMBE ARCHIVE)

The transcript of the expenses involved in dealing with this body from Figure 7-21 is shown below:

An Accoumpt of our Disburstm^t Concerning Thomas Greep

p^d for the Coroners ffee [£]0 13[s] 4[d]

p^d John Smerdon of Rowdon for Riding to Exeter to fetch the Coroner 0 5[s] 0

p^d in Expences at Widecombe Town when the Coroner was here 0 3[s] 0

p^d in Expences when Thomas Greeps Goods was Sold 0 1[s] 6[d]

p^d for Two men to watch by Tho: Greep after he was found Dead for Two Dayes Each man 1s p day Comes to 0 4[s] 0
And for Three men to watch by him by Night for Two Nights time at 1s-6d Each man Each night Comes to 0 9[s] 0

p^d Roger Hannaford for One Seames of wood which was Burnt by the watchmen 0 1[s] 6[d]
and for Straw Made use of by the watchmen 0 0 0½[d]

So, someone had to travel to Exeter on horseback to fetch the coroner. Once in Widecombe, the coroner had to be entertained, and his fee had to be paid. The body had to be watched over, presumably until burial, or at least until the coroner had reached his conclusions as to cause of death, and the watchers had to be kept warm while they did it. Overall, an expensive business, and this would apply whether or not Thomas Greep was of the parish.

BURIALS IN WOOL

The Burying in Woollen Acts 1666-80 were Acts of the Parliament of England which required the dead, except plague victims and the destitute, to be buried in pure English woollen shrouds to the exclusion of any foreign textiles.

It was a requirement that an affidavit be sworn in front of a Justice of the Peace (usually by a relative of the deceased), confirming burial in wool, with the punishment of a £5 fee for non-compliance[45]. A different source explains the reason behind this ruling, indicating that its aims were "for the lessening the importation of linen from beyond the seas, and the encouragement of the woollen and paper manufacturer of the kingdom."[46]

Given the Overseers' responsibility for the dead in their care we can see the relevance of the following extract from A003.p008 (Figure 7-22):

---

[45] Reference: https://en.wikipedia.org/wiki/Burying_in_Woollen_Acts.

[46] Reference: http://www.historyhouse.co.uk/articles/buried_in_wool.html.

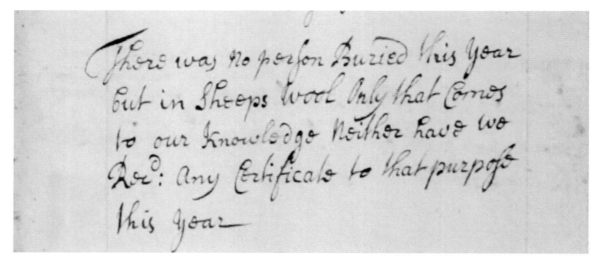

FIGURE 7-22: DETAIL FROM THE OVERSEERS' ACCOUNTS FOR 1734/5 CONCERNING THE PRACTICE OF BURYING THE DEAD IN WOOL

(IMAGE A003.P008 FROM THE WIDECOMBE ARCHIVE)

The transcript of the extract in Figure 7-22 is as follows:

There was no person Buried this year but in Sheeps Wool Only that Comes to our Knowledge Neither have we Rec^d Any Certificate to that purpose this year

BURYING ROBERT FRENCH

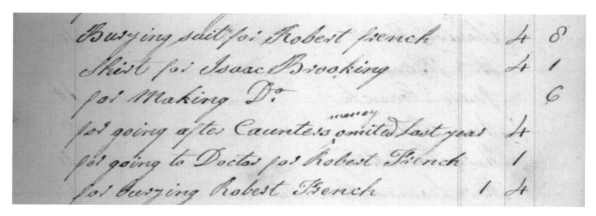

FIGURE 7-23: DETAIL FROM THE OVERSEERS' ACCOUNTS FOR 1814/5 CONCERNING THE BURIAL SUIT FOR ROBERT FRENCH AND THE COSTS OF BURIAL

(IMAGE A007.005.P011 FROM THE WIDECOMBE ARCHIVE)

In 1814-15 the Overseers were paying 4s 8d for a *"burying suit"* for Robert French (see Figure 7-23). They were also paying the expenses of burying him: *"for going to Doctor"* 1s and for burying him £1 4s.

Later that same year they were paying the costs of burying Richard Hamlyn.

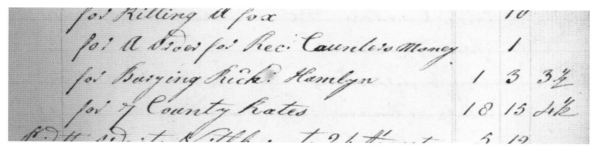

FIGURE 7-24: DETAIL FROM THE OVERSEERS' ACCOUNTS FOR 1814/5 CONCERNING THE COSTS OF BURIAL OF RICHARD HAMLYN

(IMAGE A007.005.P015 FROM THE WIDECOMBE ARCHIVE)

The transcription of the entry in Figure 7-24 is as follows:

for burying Richd Hamlyn [£]1 3[s] 3½[d]

MONEY FROM DEAD BODIES

Money was also taken from the bodies of dead people found on the moor (yes, unlike today, unfortunately it was not that uncommon to come across a dead body on the moor). Dealing with such bodies was the responsibility of the parish and the costs would come out of the Overseers' funds, so it seems only fair that if the dead had money on his or her person then that should be appropriated.

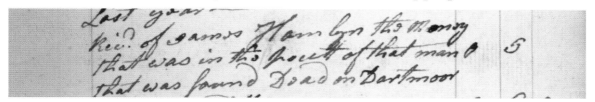

FIGURE 7-25: DETAIL FROM THE OVERSEERS' ACCOUNTS FOR 1801 CONCERNING THE APPROPRIATION OF MONEY FOUND IN THE POCKET OF A DEAD PERSON

(IMAGE A006.002.P028 FROM THE WIDECOMBE ARCHIVE)

The transcription of the entry in Figure 7-25 is as follows:

*Rec^d of James Hamlyn the money
That was in the pocett of that man
That was found Dead on Dartmoor [£]0 5[s]*

BASTARDY

ALLOCATING RESPONSIBILITY

It is unfortunate that we have to single out this particular status of an individual, but it was enshrined in the legislation and an integral part of the system of poor relief so we should consider it. The Overseers' responsibility is, in part, to ensure that money spent from the Poor Rate is legitimately spent on appropriate relief. It follows that a woman with a young child with no means of support would be a just recipient of relief. It also follows that if a father can be identified and brought to account then that father should pay his fair share of that relief to the overall reduction of the Poor Rate. So part, at least, of the Overseers' duty was to make sure that this happened whenever possible.

As Webb 1927 page 308 put it: "A special activity of the zealous parish officer was his attempt to indemnify the parish at the cost of private individuals for the expense of maintaining particular paupers. This activity was practically confined to the case of illegitimate children, the family connections of ordinary paupers being usually themselves too nearly destitute to be worth proceeding against for contribution towards their support."

And, further, on page 309: "The timely discovery of unmarried women with child; the cajoling, persuading or intimidating them to 'swear' the expected child to some man, preferably one of substantial means; the bargaining with that person, under threat of immediate apprehension, for a lump sum down, or an undertaking for a weekly contribution - all this noisome business formed part of the duties of the Overseer of the Poor [......] No further evidence of fatherhood than the woman's oath was required for the issue of a warrant against the putative father". This can be seen to easily lead to corruption of one form or another, some of which is related by Webb, but it can be hopefully agreed that pursuing this line of enquiry is beyond the scope of the present document and may well have been primarily an urban rather than a rural issue in any case.

Again, on page 311: "in most parishes it was the custom of the Overseers to pay 'to the mother of a bastard the sum directed by the order of maintenance, whether it be recovered from the father or not; and this comes under the denomination of 'pay' in pauper language. The sum allowed to the mother of a bastard [under a magistrate's order] is generally greater than that given [as Outdoor Relief] to the mother of a legitimate child; indeed the whole treatment of the former is a direct encouragement to vice'"[47].

Webb concludes by remarking that women who had three or four illegitimate children in succession became entitled to a pension of ten or fifteen shillings per week. Such a sum, paid regularly by the parish, was often more than the whole earnings of a rural labourer, so it might be accepted that the income to be made under such a bastardy law was actually '*a loadstone to draw women into a state of pregnancy*'[48]. This of course rather ignores the role of men in all of this but it was the

---

[47] From the report of Poor Law Inquiry Commissioners, Appendix A, Majendie's Report p. 165.

[48] Quoted from the report of Poor Law Inquiry Commissioners, Appendix C page 355 (Mortimer's letter).

lot of the women to look after these children and men's role was reduced to paying a regular allowance to maintain them, if they were so able.

There are many cases of payments made to women in the Widecombe Overseers' Accounts, annotated with 'BC' to signify that it was a payment relating to a 'bastard child' or 'base child'. See, for example Figure 7-4 in the section on "Spending the Poor Rate' above. There are also cases of payments for confinement prior to the birth.

BASE CHILDREN

A related matter concerns the birth of a base (or bastard) child to a poor mother that would normally become the responsibility of the home parish of the mother. There was a warrant issued in 1830 for a George Lake of Exeter who was charged with being the father of Susan Lamble Hamlyn's child (see Figure 7-27). The warrant was issued to instruct the 'Peace Officers' to apprehend him to obtain indemnity against the charge falling to Widecombe. Note that this is a printed document which suggests this matter was not that unusual.

Local action was also taken as evidenced in Figure 7-26.

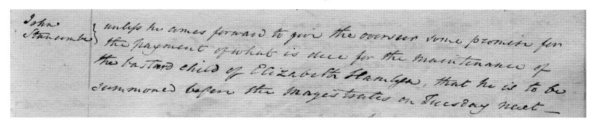

FIGURE 7-26: DECEMBER 14TH 1821 MINUTE RECORDING THE SUMMONS OF JOHN STANCOMBE IN THE WIDECOMBE SELECT VESTRY MINUTE BOOK

(DOCUMENT 2955A/PV/1 FROM THE SW HERITAGE TRUST DEVON ARCHIVES)

The transcript of Figure 7-26 is as follows:

John Stancombe
unless he comes forward to give the overseer some promise for
the payment of what is due for the Maintenance of
the bastard child of Elizabeth Hamlyn, that he is to be
summoned before the Magistrates on Tuesday next.

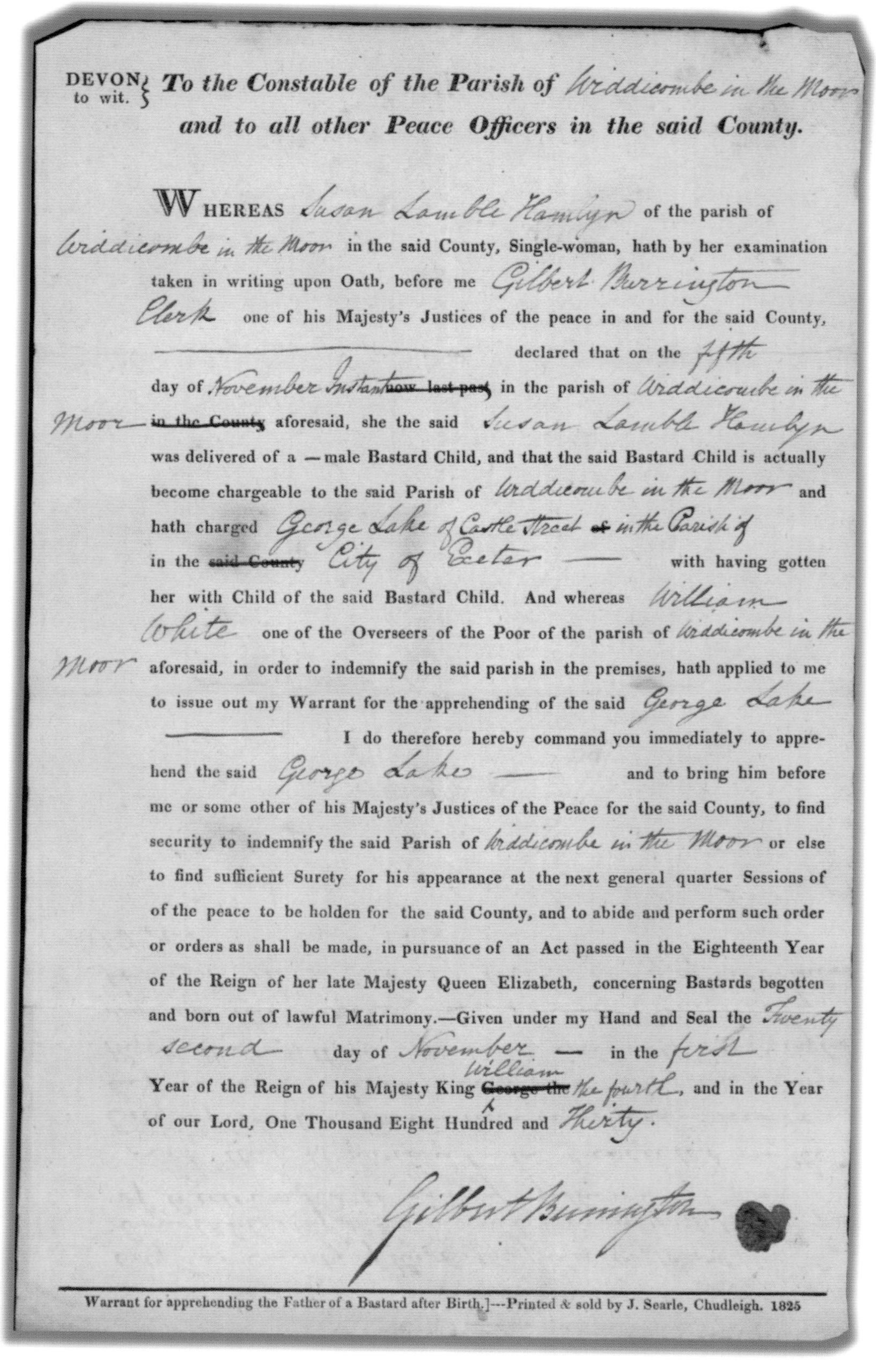

FIGURE 7-27: WARRANT FOR THE APPREHENSION OF GEORGE LAKE, PURPORTED FATHER OF SUSAN LAMBLE HAMLYN'S BASTARD CHILD

(IMAGE A052A.603.F FROM THE WIDECOMBE ARCHIVE)

The transcript of the form shown in Figure 7-27 is as follows:

DEVON to wit.} To the Constable of the Parish of Widdicombe in the Moor
*   and to all other Peace Officers in the said County.*
Whereas Susan Lamble Hamlyn of the parish of
Widdicombe in the Moor in the said County, Single-woman hath by her examination
taken in writing upon Oath, before me Gilbert Burrington
Clerk one of his Majesty's Justices of the peace in and for the said County,
declared that on the fifth day of November Instant now last past in the parish of
Widdicombe in the
Moor in the County aforesaid, she the said Susan Lamble Hamlyn
was delivered of a - male Bastard Child, and that the said Bastard Child is actually
become chargeable to the said Parish of Widdecombe in the Moor and
hath charged George Lake of Castle Street in the Parish of
in the City of Exeter with having gotten
her with Child of the said Bastard Child. And whereas William
White one of the Overseers of the Poor of the parish of Widdicombe in the
Moor aforesaid, in order to indemnify the said parish in the premises, hath applied
to me
to issue out my Warrant for the apprehending of the said George Lake
I do therefore hereby command you immediately to appre-
hend the said George Lake and to bring him before
me or some other of his Majesty's Justices of the Peace for the said County, to find
security to indemnify the said Parish of Widdicombe in the Moor or else
to find sufficient Surety for his appearance at the next general quarter Sessions of
of the peace to be holden for the said County, and to abide and perform such order
or orders as shall be made, in pursuance of an Act passed in the Eighteenth Year
of the Reign of her late Majesty Queen Elizabeth, concerning Bastards begotten
and born out of Lawful Matrimony. -Given under my Hand and Seal the Twenty
Second day of November in the first
Year of the Reign of his Majesty King William the fourth, and in the Year
of our Lord, One Thousand Eight Hundred and Thirty.
Gilbert Burrington
Warrant for apprehending the Father of a Bastard after Birth]---Printed and sold by
J. Searle, Chudleigh. 1825

CHAPTER 8 THE APPRENTICESHIP SYSTEM

A gap left by the previous chapter is that of children and their employment. Presumably there was some, even if minimal, provision for education and this is considered in a bit more detail in Chapter 11, but aside from that, the Churchwardens and Overseers were empowered by the Act of 1601 to bind any children *"whose parents they judge not able to maintain them, to be apprenticed where they think fit, till such man child come to the age of twenty-four, and such woman child to the age of twenty-one or marriage"*[49]. A premium was often paid to the employer, although in Widecombe, even though there are some payments, the practice does not appear to have been universally adopted.

"Throughout the whole of the eighteenth century we find constant complaints of the indifference of Churchwardens and Overseers to anything beyond saving the parish the keep of the boy or girl". In 1732 a writer denounced the "very bad practice in parish officers who, to save expense, are apt to ruin children, by putting them out as early as they can, to any sorry masters that will take them, without any concern for their education or welfare, on account of the little money that is given with them"[50].

From 1692 onwards, by a statute enacted in that year, duly indentured apprentices acquired a settlement in the parish in which they served and were thereby effectively removed from their original 'home' parish[51]. This provided a further incentive to Overseers to apprentice children out, and especially to a master in another parish, as any future liability was thereby diminished. Of course, Overseers in other parishes had the same idea and might well place children in Widecombe, so overall the effects might cancel out. We can see the effect of this in the attempt to remove Mary Hamlyn and her family of six children from Stoke Damerel to Widecombe because her husband had been apprenticed there (see A052.386a and A052.386a2 - in Chapter 9 on Removal Orders).

Furthermore, Dr Burn writing in 1764 described it as one of the chief duties of an Overseer as commonly understood, "to bind out poor children apprentice, no matter to whom or to what trade, but to take special care that the master live in another parish"[52]. Sixty years later the Report of the Poor Law Enquiry Commission was

---

[49] This is quoted in Webb 1927, page 196.

[50] From "An Account of the Workhouse in Great Britain in the year 1732" quoted in Webb 1927, page 198.

[51] Ibid., page 199.

[52] Ibid., page 199.

saying "when I enquired of the Assistant Overseer of the borough…how the apprentices turned out after they were bound, his answer was 'We have nothing to do with them afterwards'"[53].

The mind boggles as to the fate of the majority of these children. By 1800 some more control was being exercised with the Justices of the Peace taking much more responsibility to satisfy themselves of the suitability of the master to take the apprentices[54].

Towards the end of the eighteenth century a new practice seemed to be emerging: that of drafting children out to employers in the parish by rotation or by drawing of lots, or by arbitrary placement among the parishioners. Whichever method was used the aim was to spread the load evenly amongst the parishioners. In Widecombe there are preserved records of upwards of five hundred of these apprenticeships, and this may not of course be all of them. Even though the records cover a period of two hundred years or so, the majority of the apprenticeships for which records survive seem to be post 1780.

After October 1816 all children bound as apprentices had to be at least 9 years old. There is a child Robert Hannaford aged 9 in the archive who, in 1817, has been confirmed to be of the required age before being allowed to be bound (see Figure 8-1).

The archive also has Robert Hannaford's apprentice indenture (Widecombe Archive reference A052.398a - see Figure 8-2). This shows he was apprenticed to John Hannaford on the same day as the age verification above.

---

[53] Webb 1927, page 199.

[54] Ibid., page 205.

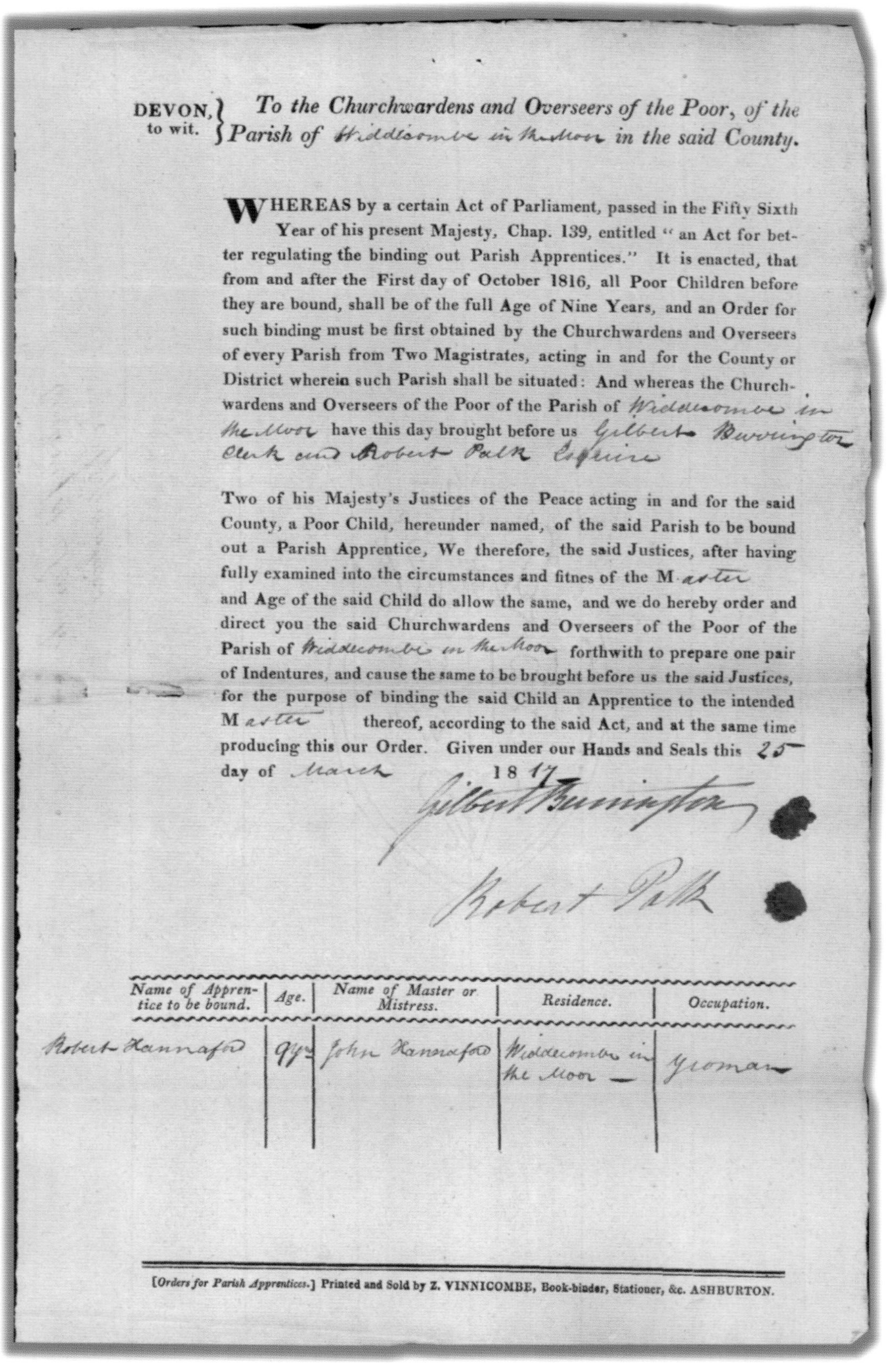

DEVON,) To the Churchwardens and Overseers of the Poor, of the
to wit. } Parish of *Widdicombe in the Moor* in the said County.

WHEREAS by a certain Act of Parliament, passed in the Fifty Sixth
Year of his present Majesty, Chap. 139, entitled " an Act for better regulating the binding out Parish Apprentices.'' It is enacted, that
from and after the First day of October 1816, all Poor Children before
they are bound, shall be of the full Age of Nine Years, and an Order for
such binding must be first obtained by the Churchwardens and Overseers
of every Parish from Two Magistrates, acting in and for the County or
District wherein such Parish shall be situated: And whereas the Churchwardens and Overseers of the Poor of the Parish of *Widdicombe in
the Moor* have this day brought before us *Gilbert Burrington
Clerk and Robert Palk Esquire*

Two of his Majesty's Justices of the Peace acting in and for the said
County, a Poor Child, hereunder named, of the said Parish to be bound
out a Parish Apprentice, We therefore, the said Justices, after having
fully examined into the circumstances and fitnes of the M *aster*
and Age of the said Child do allow the same, and we do hereby order and
direct you the said Churchwardens and Overseers of the Poor of the
Parish of *Widdicombe in the Moor* forthwith to prepare one pair
of Indentures, and cause the same to be brought before us the said Justices,
for the purpose of binding the said Child an Apprentice to the intended
M *aster* thereof, according to the said Act, and at the same time
producing this our Order. Given under our Hands and Seals this *25*
day of *March* , 18 *17*

Name of Appren-tice to be bound.	Age.	Name of Master or Mistress.	Residence.	Occupation.
Robert Hannaford	9½	John Hannaford	Widdecombe in the Moor	Yeoman

[*Orders for Parish Apprentices.*] Printed and Sold by Z. VINNICOMBE, Book-binder, Stationer, &c. ASHBURTON.

FIGURE 8-1: 1817 DOCUMENT CONFIRMING THE VERIFICATION OF THE CIRCUMSTANCES OF THE APPRENTICESHIP AND THE AGE OF ROBERT HANNAFORD

(IMAGE A052.398B.F FROM THE WIDECOMBE ARCHIVE)

The Apprenticeship System

The transcription of the document in Figure 8-1 is as follows:

DEVON, to wit
To the Churchwardens and Overseers of the Poor, of the
Parish of Widdicombe in the Moor in the said County.
Whereas by a certain Act of Parliament, passed in the Fifty Sixth
Year of his present Majesty, Chap. 139 entitled "an Act for bet-
ter regulating the Binding out Parish Apprentices." It is enacted, that
from and after the first day of October 1816, all Poor Children before
they are bound, shall be of the full Age of Nine Years, and an Order for
such binding must be first obtained by the Churchwardens and Overseers
of every Parish from Two Magistrates, acting in and for the County or
District wherein such Parish shall be situated: and whereas the Church -
wardens and Overseers of the Poor of the Parish of Widdecombe in
the Moor here this day brought before us Gilbert Burrington
Clerk and Robert Palk Esquire
Two of his Majesty's Justices of the Peace acting in and for the said
County, a Poor Child hereunder named, of the said Parish to be bound
out a Parish Apprentice, We therefore, the said Justices, after having
fully examined into the circumstances and fitnes of the Master
and Age of the said Child do allow the same, and we do hereby order and

direct you the said Churchwardens and Overseers of the Poor of the
Parish of Widdecombe in the Moor forthwith to prepare one pair
of Indentures, and cause the same to be brought before us the said Justices,
for the purpose of binding the said Child an Apprentice to the intended
Master thereof, according to the said Act, and at the same time
producing this our Order. Given under our Hands and Seals this 25
day of March 1817
Gilbert Burrington
Robert Palk

Name of Apprentice to be bound: Robert Hannaford
Age: 9yrs
Name of Master or Mistress: John Hannaford
Residence: Widdecombe in the Moor
Occupation: Yeoman

[Orders for Parish Apprentices.] Printed and Sold by Z. VINNICOMBE, Book-binder,
Stationer, a&c. AS

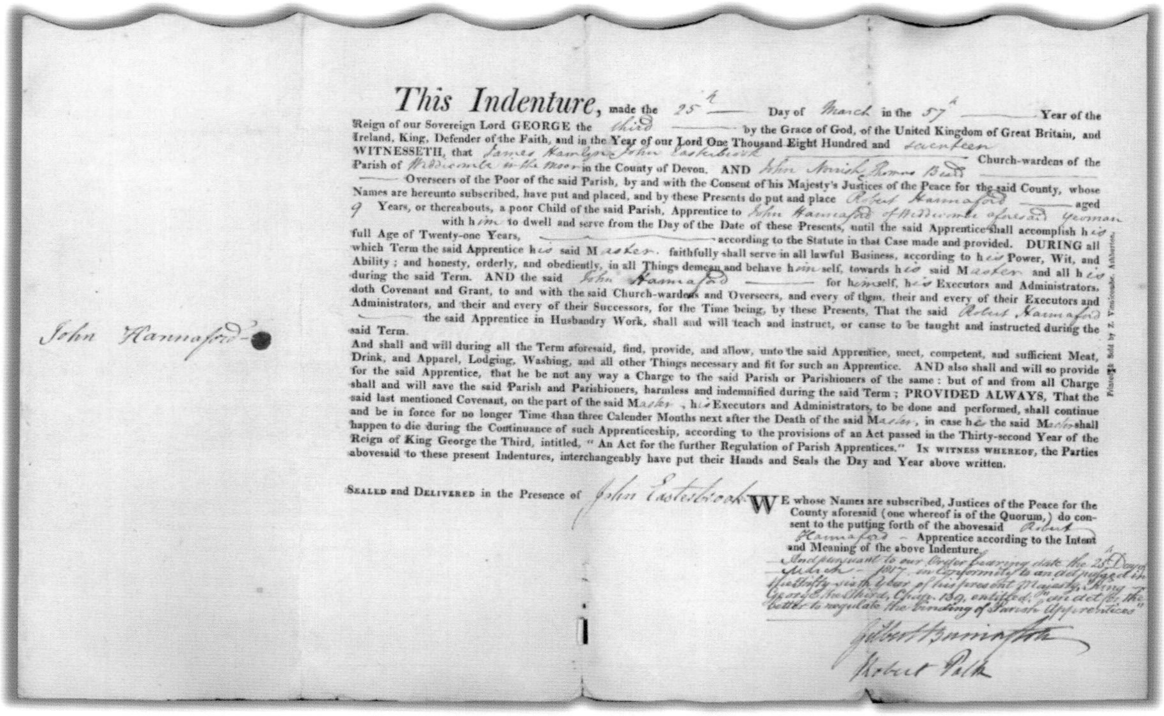

John Hannaford

This Indenture, made the 25th Day of March in the 57th Year of the Reign of our Sovereign Lord GEORGE the third by the Grace of God, of the United Kingdom of Great Britain, and Ireland, King, Defender of the Faith, and in the Year of our Lord One Thousand Eight Hundred and seventeen WITNESSETH, that James Hamlyn John Easterbrook Church-wardens of the Parish of Widdecombe in the moor in the County of Devon, AND John Norrish Thomas Beard Overseers of the Poor of the said Parish, by and with the Consent of his Majesty's Justices of the Peace for the said County, whose Names are hereunto subscribed, have put and placed, and by these Presents do put and place Robert Hannaford aged 9 Years, or thereabouts, a poor Child of the said Parish, Apprentice to John Hannaford of Widdecombe aforesaid Yeoman with him to dwell and serve from the Day of the Date of these Presents, until the said Apprentice shall accomplish his full Age of Twenty-one Years, according to the Statute in that Case made and provided. DURING all which Term the said Apprentice his said Master faithfully shall serve in all lawful Business, according to his Power, Wit, and Ability; and honesty, orderly, and obediently, in all Things demean and behave himself, towards his said Master and all his during the said Term. AND the said John Hannaford for himself, his Executors and Administrators, doth Covenant and Grant, to and with the said Church-wardens and Overseers, and every of them, their and every of their Executors and Administrators, and their and every of their Successors, for the Time being, by these Presents, That the said Robert Hannaford the said Apprentice in Husbandry Work, shall and will teach and instruct, or cause to be taught and instructed during the said Term.
And shall and will during all the Term aforesaid, find, provide, and allow, unto the said Apprentice, meet, competent, and sufficient Meat, Drink, and Apparel, Lodging, Washing, and all other Things necessary and fit for such an Apprentice. AND also shall and will so provide for the said Apprentice, that he be not any way a Charge to the said Parish or Parishioners of the same: but of and from all Charge shall and will save the said Parish and Parishioners, harmless and indemnified during the said Term; PROVIDED ALWAYS, That the said last mentioned Covenant, on the part of the said Master, his Executors and Administrators, to be done and performed, shall continue and be in force for no longer Time than three Calender Months next after the Death of the said Master, in case he the said Master shall happen to die during the Continuance of such Apprenticeship, according to the provisions of an Act passed in the Thirty-second Year of the Reign of King George the Third, intitled, "An Act for the further Regulation of Parish Apprentices." IN WITNESS WHEREOF, the Parties abovesaid to these present Indentures, interchangeably have put their Hands and Seals the Day and Year above written.

SEALED and DELIVERED in the Presence of John Easterbrook

WE whose Names are subscribed, Justices of the Peace for the County aforesaid (one whereof is of the Quorum,) do consent to the putting forth of the abovesaid Robert Hannaford Apprentice according to the Intent and Meaning of the above Indenture.
And pursuant to our Order bearing date the 25th Day of March 1817, in Conformity to an Act passed in the fifty sixth Year of his present Majesty King George the Third, Chap. 139, entitled, "An Act for the better to regulate the binding of Parish Apprentices"

Gilbert Burrington
Robert Polk

Printed & Sold by Z. Vinnicombe, Ashburton.

FIGURE 8-2: 1817 INDENTURE CONCERNING THE APPRENTICESHIP OF ROBERT HANNAFORD TO JOHN HANNAFORD

(IMAGE A052.398A.F FROM THE WIDECOMBE ARCHIVE)

PAYMENTS TO TAKE APPRENTICES

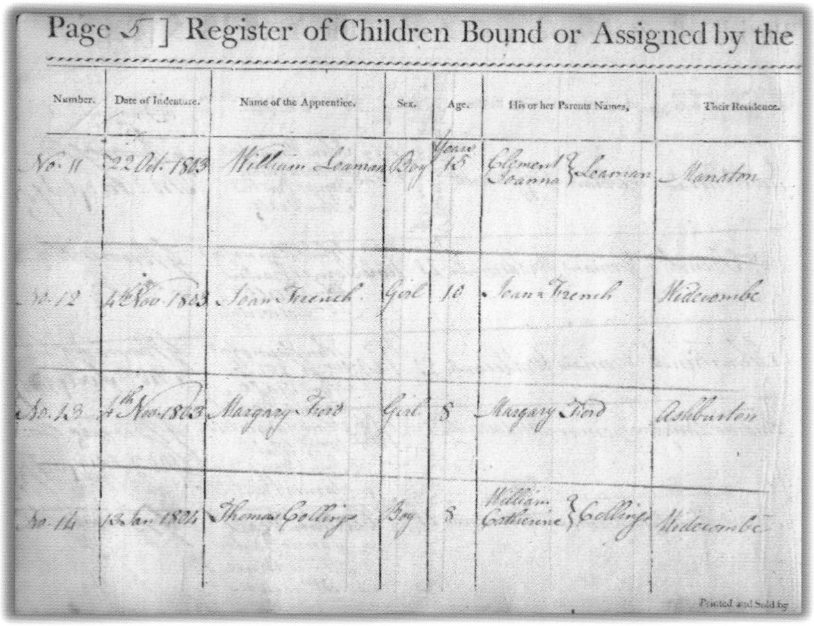

Page 5] Register of Children Bound or Assigned by the

Number.	Date of Indenture.	Name of the Apprentice.	Sex.	Age.	His or her Parents Names,	Their Residence.
No. 11	22 Oct. 1803	William Leaman	Boy	Years 15	Clement & Joanna Leaman	Manaton
No. 12	4th Nov. 1803	Joan French	Girl	10	Joan French	Widecombe
No. 13	4th Nov. 1803	Margery Ford	Girl	8	Margery Ford	Ashburton
No. 14	13 Jan 1804	Thomas Collings	Boy	8	William & Catherine Collings	Widecombe

Printed and Sold by

FIGURE 8-3: PAGE 5, LEFT-HAND-SIDE OF THE 1803 REGISTER OF CHILDREN BOUND OR ASSIGNED

(IMAGE A011.005.P005 FROM THE WIDECOMBE ARCHIVE)

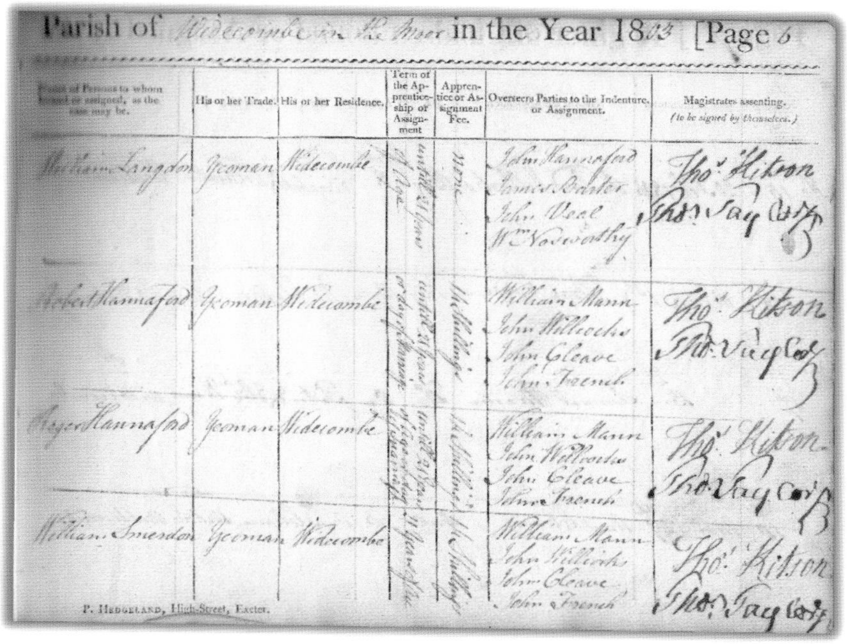

FIGURE 8-4: PAGE 5, RIGHT-HAND-SIDE OF THE 1803 REGISTER OF CHILDREN BOUND OR ASSIGNED

(IMAGE A011.005.P006 FROM THE WIDECOMBE ARCHIVE)

It is not generally clear from the Overseers' Accounts whether fees were paid to the employers as a matter of course (although there are numerous examples of the practice in the Accounts). However, in the Register of Children Bound or Assigned by the Parish of Widecombe-in-the-Moor, e.g. A011.005.p005 and p006 (see Figure 8-3 and Figure 8-4), there is a column headed 'Apprentice or Assignment Fee' and this shows e.g. 14 shillings as the fee to take Thomas Collins and there are two other entries on that page that also record fees.

Note that both William Leaman and Margary Ford originated from outside the parish of Widecombe (Manaton and Ashburton respectively), illustrating the tendency to place apprentices in neighbouring parishes. However, there is a Margery Ford being paid in the Widecombe Overseers' Accounts for that year, which could be the same person.

Also note that Joan French and Margary Ford have parents listed with the same names as them. This might indicate they are orphans, or that their mother has the same name and there is no father. Joan French is also a recipient of relief in the Overseers' Accounts. It is not always possible to obtain the names of the parents of apprenticed children. This is where the Register is so valuable. However there is only one Register in the Chest that we know of and this only covers the period 1802 - 1839.[55]

---

[55] Reference A011 in the Widecombe Archive, catalogued under 'Parish Apprenticeships'.

Finally, it should be noted that name variations were common, often written as they were heard, or subjectively understood.

THOMAS COLLINS

The apprenticeship indenture of Thomas Collins (Figure 8-5) is of interest as it tells us something of the obligations and duties of both the apprentice and the master. In particular, the child has all of his keep provided during the term of the apprenticeship but no pay is provided, or at least none is stipulated in the indenture document.

Thomas, aged 8 ('or thereabouts'), was apprenticed to William Smerdon of Lower Natsworthy until he reached the age of twenty-one.

"DURING all which Term the said Apprentice his said Master faithfully shall serve in all lawful Businesses, according to his Power, Wit, and Ability; and honestly, orderly, and obediently in all Things demean and behave him self towards his said Master and all his during the said Term." Thomas will be instructed *"in husbandry Work"* and his Master *"shall and will teach, and instruct, or cause to be taught and instructed, in the best Way and Manner that he can."* As payment Thomas' Master will *"find, provide, and allow unto the said Apprentice meet, competent, and sufficient Meat, Drink, Apparel, Lodging, Washing, and other Things necessary and fit for an Apprentice".*

There is also mention that the child shall not be a burden on the parish during the term of the apprenticeship. However, there is no mention of suits of clothing provided at the end of the term as there is with Samuel Leaman below.

Study of the Overseers' Accounts for the period (1803-4) shows that prior to the seventh month of that year, the parish was paying William Collins (or Collings) four or five shillings monthly for his son.[56] There is also an entry for a change of clothes.[57] However, from the tenth month onwards the entry has no money against it and by the end of the year William Collins has disappeared from the Accounts entirely.

---

[56] See for instance A006.005.p013 in the Widecombe Archive.

[57] See A006.005.p009 in the Widecombe Archive.

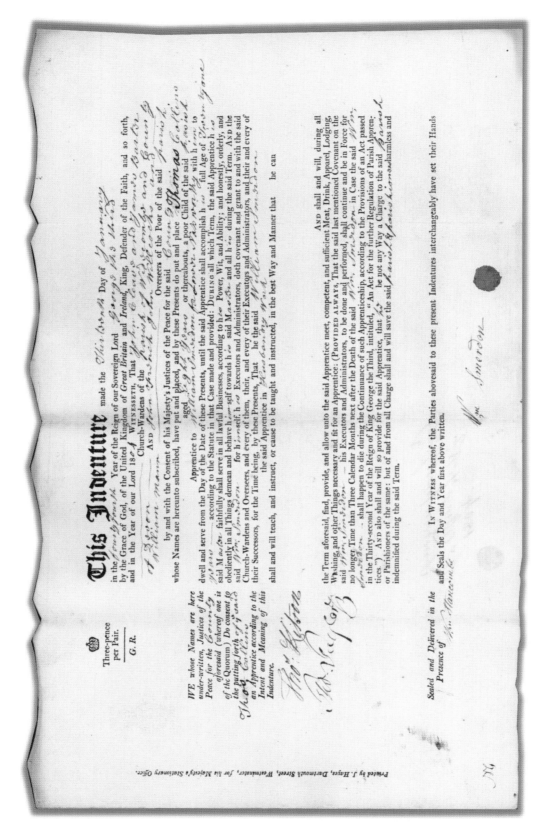

FIGURE 8-5: 1804 INDENTURE RECORDING THE BINDING AS AN APPRENTICE OF THOMAS COLLINS AGED 8 YEARS

(IMAGE A052.260.F FROM THE WIDECOMBE ARCHIVE)

SAMUEL LEAMAN

Samuel was placed in 1741 with John Torr a Yeoman from Widecombe from that date (his age is not specified) until he reached the age of twenty-four (Figure 8-6). He did not receive any (specified) wages but was to be instructed in "*Good Husbandry*" and kept with "*meet, competent, and sufficient Meat, Drink and Apparel, Lodging, Washing, and all other Things necessary and fit for an Apprentice*".

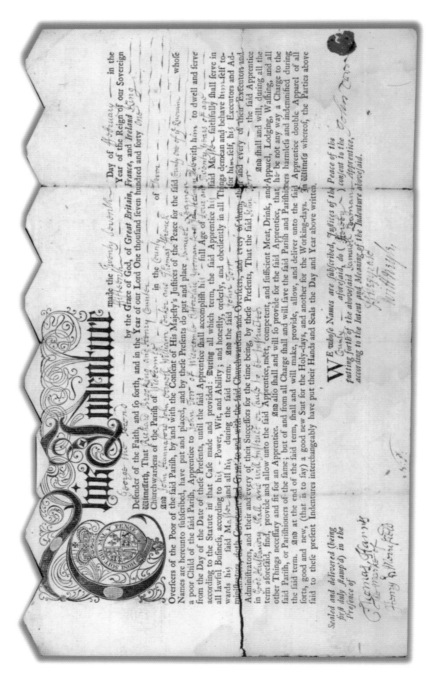

FIGURE 8-6: 1741 INDENTURE RECORDING THE BINDING AS AN APPRENTICE OF SAMUEL LEAMAN

(IMAGE A052.044.F FROM THE WIDECOMBE ARCHIVE)

The transcription of Figure 8-6 is worth reproducing in full as it shows the rules and regulations of the time.

This Indenture made the Twenty Seventh Day of ffebruary in the
Ffifteenth Year of the Reign of our Sovereign
George the Second by the Grace of God, of Great Britain, France, and Ireland King
Defender of the Faith, and so forth and in the Year of our Lord One thousand seven
hundred and forty one
Witnesseth, That Richard Brooking and Henry Caunter
Churchwardens of the Parish of Widecombe in the County of Devon
and John Hannaford John Arnell William Coaker and Thomas ffrench
Overseers of the Poor of the said Parish, by and with the consent of His Majesty's
Justices of the Peace for the said County one of ye Quorum whose
Names are hereunto subscribed, have put and placed, and by these Presents do put
and place Samuel Leaman
a poor Child of the said Parish, Apprentice to John Torr of Widecombe afforesaid
Yeoman for John Holman Hale with him to dwell and serve
from the Day of the Date of these Presents, until the said Apprentice shall
accomplish his full Age of four and Twenty Years of age
according to the Statute in that Case made and provided: During all which term, the
said Apprentice his said Master faithfully shall serve in
all lawful Business, according to his -Power, Wit and Ability; and honestly, orderly,
and obediently in all Things demean and behave himself to-
wards his said Master and all his during the said term. And the said John Torr for
himself, his Executors and Ad-
ministrators doth Covenant and Grant to and with the said Churchwardens and
Overseers, and every of them, their and each of their Executors and
Administrators, and their and every of their Successors for the time being, by these
Presents, That the said John Torr the said Apprentice
in Good Husbandry Shall and will Instruct or Cause to be instructed And shall and
will, during all the
term aforesaid, find provide and allow unto the said Apprentice, meet competent,
and sufficient Meat, Drink and Apparel, Lodging, Washing, and all
other Things necessary and fit for an Apprentice. And also shall and will so provide
for the said Apprentice, that he be not any way a Charge to the
said Parish, or Parishioners of the same; but of and from all Charge shall and will
save the said Parish and Parishioners harmless and indemnified during
the said term. And at the end of the said term, shall and will make, provide, allow
and deliver unto the said Apprentice double Apparel of all
sorts, good and new, (that is to say) a good new Suit for the Holy-days, and another
for the Working-days. In Witness whereof, the Parties above
said to these present Indentures interchangeably have put their Hands and Seals the
Day and Year above written.
WE whose Names are subscribed, Justices of the Peace of the
County aforesaid do (Hereby-) consent to the
putting forth of the abovesaid Samuell Leaman - Apprentice,
according to the Intent and Meaning of the Indenture abovesaid.

sealed and delivered (being
first duly stamp'd) in the
Presence of
Thomas, Harris
the Marke of
Henry h Merrifield
John Torr

Note especially that Samuel shall not become a charge to the parish during the period of his apprenticeship and that at the end of the term he is to have two good suits: one for holy-days and one for working-days. Note also that no parents are specified.

ELIAS NORRISH

Another indication of payments that were agreed as part of the apprenticeship negotiation is evidenced by the document in Figure 8-7. Elias Norrish was apparently 'incapable of Farm labour' and so was to be apprenticed as a Cordwainer.

The transcription of Figure 8-7 is as follows:

at a Meeting of the Parishioners held after due Notice
in the Parish Chamber this 6th day of February 1854
A Boy incapable of Farm labour named Elias Norrish
aged about Fifteen years requiring to be apprenticed
to be taught a Trade
    Presence JH Mason Vicar
            Robert Hext } Churchwardens
            Samuel Chaffe
            William Norrish Guardian
            Thomas Hannaford Overseer
            Joseph Winsor Way Warden
            James Nosworthy
Charles Warren of Ponsworthy Cordwainer being present
he agreed to take and instruct the said Elias Norrish in the
Trade of a Cordwainer upon the conditions and terms following

Paid May 5th
in the presence
of JH Mason
at the Vicarage

Elias Norrish
is hereby bound to Charles Warren of Ponsworthy to be
taught the Trade of a Boot and Shoe Maker to be clothed
fed and supported by him the said Charles Warren until

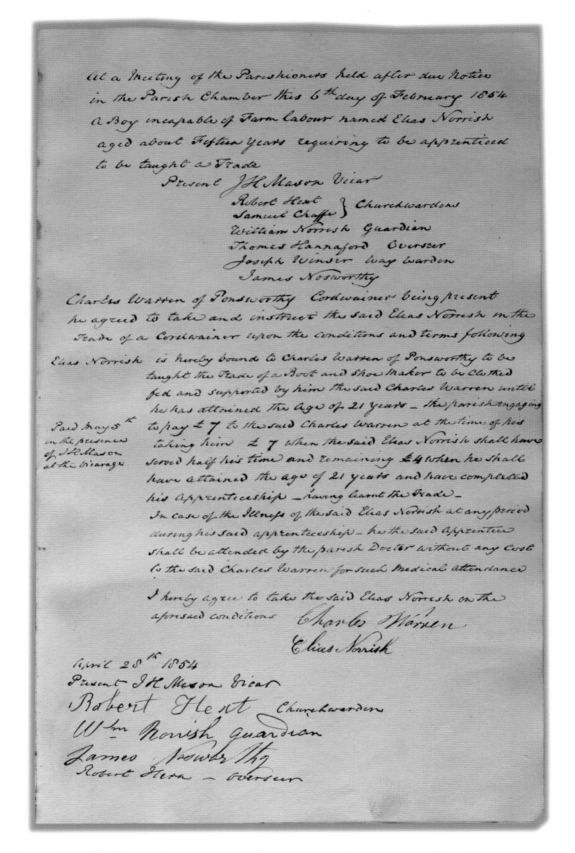

FIGURE 8-7: 1854 MINUTE RECORDING THE BINDING AS AN APPRENTICE OF ELIAS NORRISH IN THE WIDECOMBE SELECT VESTRY MINUTE BOOK

(DOCUMENT 2955A/PV/1 FROM THE SW HERITAGE TRUST DEVON ARCHIVES)

89

*he has attained the Age of 21 years - the Parish engaging
to pay £7 to the said Charles Warren at the time of his
taking him £7 when the said Elias Norrish shall have
served half his time and remaining £4 when he shall
have attained the age of 21 years and have completed
his Apprenticeship -having learnt the Trade-
In case of the Illness of the said Elias Norrish at any period
during his said Apprenticeship - he the said Apprentice
shall be attended by the Parish Doctor without any cost
to the said Charles Warren for such Medical attendance
I hereby agree to take the said Elias Norrish on the
aforesaid conditions
Charles Warren
Elias Norrish*

*April 28th 1854
Present JH Mason Vicar
Robert Hext Churchwarden
Wm Norrish guardian
James Nosworthy
Robert Hern - Overseer*

This sounds like a special case and is certainly beyond the latest date for which there are formal apprenticeship indentures in the Archive. Furthermore, it is a single page in the minute book which otherwise finishes at a much earlier date, i.e. at the time of the formation of the Newton Abbot Union (see Chapter 10). This seems another example of the caring nature of Widecombe folk for their own. Elias was clearly physically unable to do manual work and at the same time had a good writing hand (see his signature), and the option of training as a cordwainer (shoemaker) seems a very good outcome. Also although it cost the parish money (£18 if he completed the term of the apprenticeship), he would not be a further burden on the parish (unless he fell ill).

It is also worth noting from this minute that William Norrish was clearly functioning as the Guardian of the Poor for the parish (he signs himself as such) and he must have been elected to that post under the terms of the Poor Law Amendment Act 1834 (see Chapter 10 for more details). Also there was still at least one parish Overseer - Robert Hern.

KATHERINE COURTERS

Girls were as likely as boys to be apprenticed out. Their terms were slightly different. Katherine was placed with Robt Hannaford ye Elder of ye Parish of Withecome Yeoman in 1735 "*until the said Apprentice shall accomplish her full Age of Twenty one Years or ye Day of Marriage*" (see Figure 8-8). Her age at the date of the indenture is not specified. So, if she got married before the age of twenty-one she would be released from her apprenticeship early. Boys had no such 'get-out' clause.

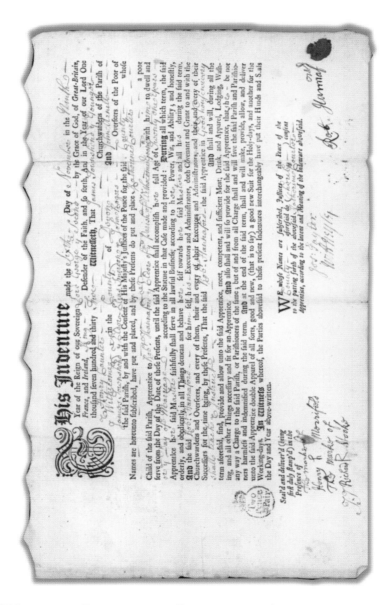

FIGURE 8-8: 1735 INDENTURE RECORDING THE BINDING AS AN APPRENTICE OF KATHERINE COURTERS

(IMAGE A052.047.F FROM THE WIDECOMBE ARCHIVE)

RESISTANCE TO APPRENTICESHIP

Those in receipt of relief or close to it were not always happy to let their children be bound as an apprentice. After all, your child would suddenly be taken from you and it is likely that thereafter you would see them only rarely. Imagine that happening today, where your child of eight or nine was, in effect, forcibly removed from your care (as still happens of course in certain cases today). The intention behind the apprenticeship system was that it offered training in a skill to children which would allow them to be usefully employed once they had grown up. Otherwise, the expectation was that they would become a burden on the parish.

In the select vestry minutes of November 30th 1821, Thomas Leaman was clearly resisting the binding of his daughter. So much so that his 'pay' was discontinued (see Figure 8-9).

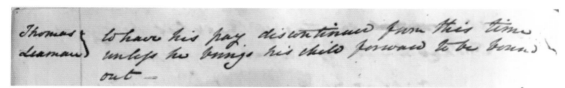

FIGURE 8-9: NOVEMBER 30TH 1821 MINUTE RECORDING THE DISCONTINUANCE OF THE PAY OF THOMAS LEAMAN IN THE WIDECOMBE SELECT VESTRY MINUTE BOOK

(DOCUMENT 2955A/PV/1 FROM THE SW HERITAGE TRUST DEVON ARCHIVES)

The transcript of Figure 8-9 is as follows:

Thomas Leaman to have his pay discontinued from this time unless he brings his child forward to be bound out

In the following meeting the matter is clearly not resolved and Thomas' wife Elizabeth is summoned before the magistrate (see Figure 8-10).

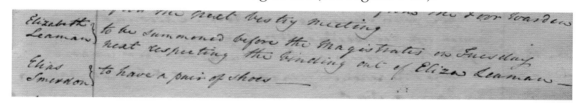

FIGURE 8-10: DECEMBER 14TH 1821 MINUTE RECORDING THE SUMMONS OF ELIZABETH LEAMAN IN THE WIDECOMBE SELECT VESTRY MINUTE BOOK

(DOCUMENT 2955A/PV/1 FROM THE SW HERITAGE TRUST DEVON ARCHIVES)

The transcript of Figure 8-10 is as follows:

Elizabeth Leaman to be summoned before the Magistrates on Tuesday next respecting the binding out of Eliza Leaman

No indenture has been found for Eliza Leaman so she may not have been bound out, although a study of later select vestry minutes may reveal more information.

CHAPTER 9 REMOVAL ORDERS

Inherent in the concept of 'Removal Orders' is the principle that everyone belonged to a parish or local community. As well as requiring obligations this also entitled the person to a level of support and protection. As Webb once again unbeatably put it:

"Every person was, as serf or as freeman, a member of some local community, to which he owed obligations, and from which he was entitled to expect some measure of protection, and, when in need, some undefined support".[58]

Anyone who found him or herself in some community other than his or her home one could be in a tricky position. Again, from Webb:

"An unknown person, absent without credentials from the community to which he belonged, was an object of grave suspicion".[59]

This is essentially the concept of 'Settlement'. Every person had a place of settlement, their 'home' parish, and travelling around was fraught with problems.

In fact, paraphrasing Webb,[60] from as early as 1662, any person[61], who, either to take a situation, or merely on a visit to relatives and friends, or for any other reason whatever, however lawful or laudable, came into a parish in which he had not a settlement, was liable - however good his character and conduct, without any application for relief or for any other gift or favour, and even after he had secured remunerative employment - unless he could give sufficient security that he would never become chargeable to the parish, to the satisfaction of the Justices - could be summarily removed in custody, together with his wife and children, under ignominious and horribly uncomfortable conditions, to whatever parish, however distant, might be believed to be the place where, according to an extremely complicated and always uncertain code of law, he had his legal settlement.

Webb (1927) further states on pages 327-8 in relation to the forcible removal of any person not belonging to the propertied class - especially any labourer or artisan, even if he had found employment at wages, and was in full vigour and good health - was liable, if found living outside the narrow bounds of the parish in which he was legally settled, to be pounced upon by the parish officers, who were incited thereto

---

[58] Webb 1927, page 315.

[59] Ibid., page 315.

[60] Ibid., page 321.

[61] Not belonging to the class of property owners which at that time numbered fewer than one-tenth of the population.

by any neighbour; and, upon a warrant usually granted as a matter of course, to be arrested and summarily packed off, with his family, in custody of the Overseer, who had to convey him to the parish in which he was believed to have a settlement.

Roger North writing about 1670 lamented that "it is a great imprisonment, if not slavery, to a poor family to be under such restraint by law that they must always live in one place, whether they have friends, kindred, employment or not, or however they might mend their condition by moving; and all because they had the ill-luck to be born or to have served or resided a certain time there".[62]

Things only moved on much later when: "The very obvious reform of not permitting the Overseer to obtain a Removal Order merely because he chose to say that he thought it 'likely' that an immigrant into his parish would, at some future date, need Poor Relief" was provided finally "by an Act of 1795 that, with the exceptions of persons deemed by law to be 'rogues and vagabonds' or 'idle and disorderly persons' and - most melancholy of all - every unmarried woman with child, no person should be liable to be removed until he had actually become chargeable to the Poor rate". The Act also provided that "if the Justice granting the order considered that such person was unable to travel by reason of sickness or other infirmity…the order was to be suspended until the Justice was satisfied that it could be executed without danger".[63] In 1809 this was extended to include the family and household of a sick or infirm person.

It is also worth noting that "to be frequently in receipt of Poor Relief was, for forty years between 1795 and 1834 the lot of nearly every farm labourer in southern England".[64] Webb goes on to describe the constant adjustments of a minor nature that were made to the legislation leading in the end to an even more arcane and complex situation than that described above.

This whole unfortunate process is evidenced in the Widecombe Parish Records through the preservation of Examination documents, with 'examination' being the process of interviewing people acquainted with or close to the individual, as well as the person themselves, to discover his or her true status, and the Removal Order which was the document ordering the removal of the individual and if applicable his or her family. One such case, that of George Leaman and his family, as an example, is considered below.

Of course, this was a two-way process, i.e. individuals could be removed FROM Widecombe to elsewhere and removed TO Widecombe from elsewhere, all with the intention of ensuring that those seeking relief did so from their legal parish.

---

[62] Quoted in Webb 1927, page 328.

[63] Ibid., page 343.

[64] Ibid., page 344.

Reflecting this, the documents in the archive show evidence of both directions of movement.

Similarly, we can view the settlement restriction from two perspectives: although it was undoubtedly a restriction, at least there was a parish that a person belonged to and could to an extent rely on for protection. We can contrast this with the situation of a refugee today who has no such luxury.

WILLIAM HANNAFORD

A straightforward case is provided by archive entry A052.383d2 which shows William Hannaford, his wife Ann and his young son John had been seeking relief from the parish of Totnes although their place of legal settlement was Widecombe (see Figure 9-1). Note the printed document, suggesting that this was a not infrequent occurrence.

INTERESTING ASIDE 3: INDENTURES

Indentures are legal contracts between two or more parties. Historically, the agreement was written twice (or more) on one sheet of paper and the copies were separated by cutting in a jagged or uneven way so that they could subsequently be put back together to prove authenticity. Where this is impractical due, for instance, to complexity, then the agreement can be written on separate sheets of paper with the cutting done along the top edges. These 'indents' in the paper are what have led to the term 'indenture' to describe these instruments, although their proper name is 'chirograph'. They occur in various places in this book.

Apprenticeship indentures are the best-known examples. See, for instance, Figure 8-5, Figure 8-6, and Figure 8-8.

The early Deed of the Customs from 1586 also uses this approach (see Figure 2-2).

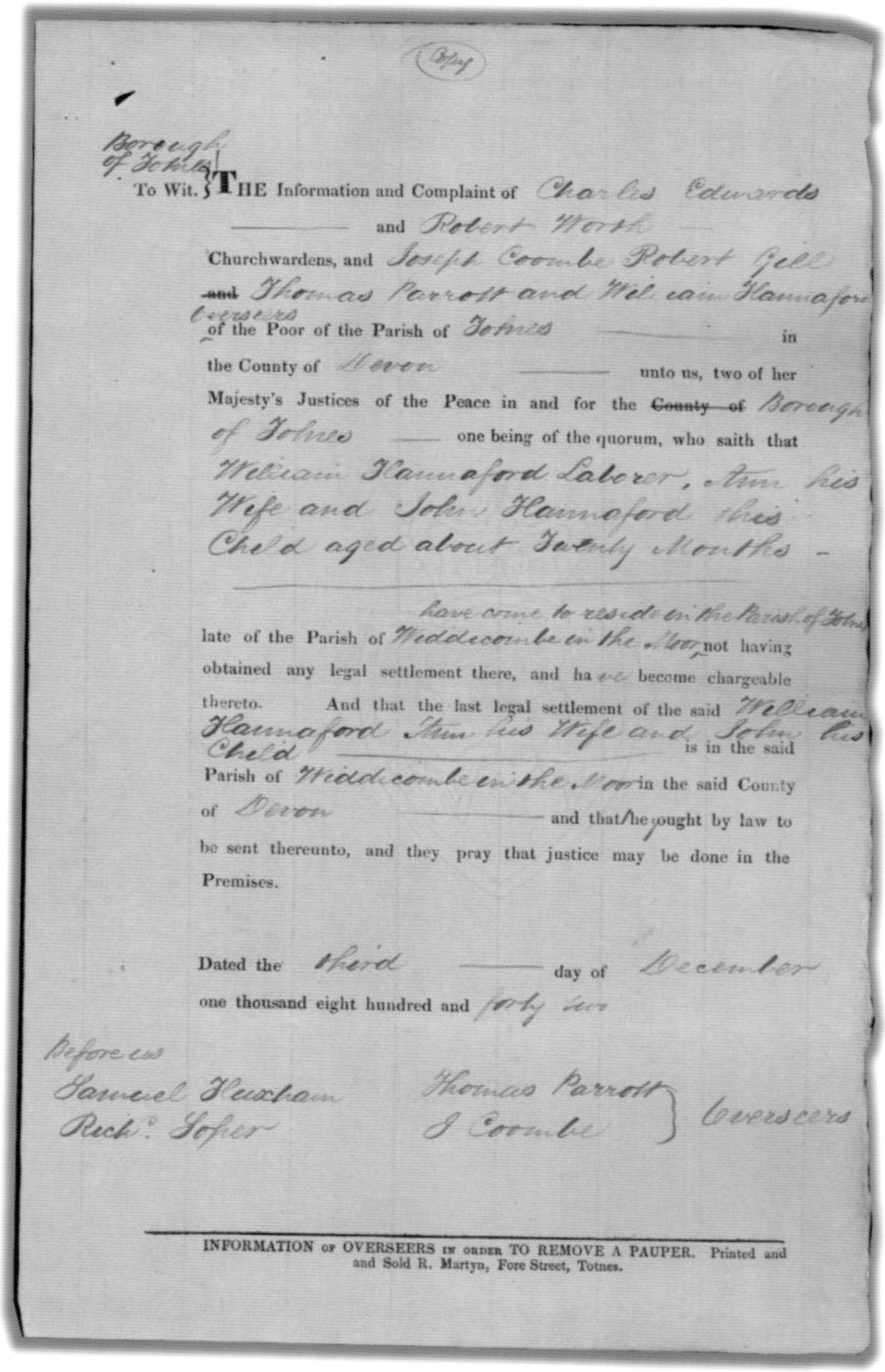

FIGURE 9-1: 1842 REMOVAL ORDER OF WILLIAM HANNAFORD AND HIS FAMILY FROM TOTNES TO WIDECOMBE

(IMAGE A052.383D2 FROM THE WIDECOMBE ARCHIVE)

The transcript of Figure 9-1 is as follows:

Borough of Totnes To Wit.
THE Information and Complaint of Charles Edwards and Robert Worth
Churchwardens, and Joseph Coombe Robert Gill
Thomas Parrott and William Hannaford
Overseers of the Poor of the Parish of Totnes in
the County of Devon unto us, two of her
Majestys Justices of the Peace in and for the Borough
of Totnes one being of the quorum who saith that
William Hannaford Laborer, Ann his
Wife and John Hannaford his
Child aged about Twenty Months
late of the Parish of Widdecombe in the Moor have come to reside in the Parish of
Totnes not having
obtained any legal settlement there and have become chargeable
thereto. And that the last legal settlement of the said William
Hannaford Ann his Wife and John his
Child is in the said
Parish of Widdicombe in the Moor in the said County
or Devon and that they ought by Law to
to sent thereunto, and they pray that justice may be done in the
Premises
dated the third day of December
one thousand eight hundred and forty two
Before us
Samuel Hexham Thomas Parrott }
Richd Soper J Coombe   } Overseers

INFORMATION OF OVERSEERS IN ORDER TO REMOVE A PAUPER. Printed and
and sold R. Martyn, Fore Street, Totnes.

MARIA HANNAFORD AND ANN POTTS (NÉE FURNIVAL)

A much more complex case is provided by the situation of Maria Hannaford and Ann Potts (née Furnival). In 1810 Ann married Charles Potts, a silk weaver and then member of the Cheshire Militia, and lived with him in Macclesfield (see Figure 9-2).

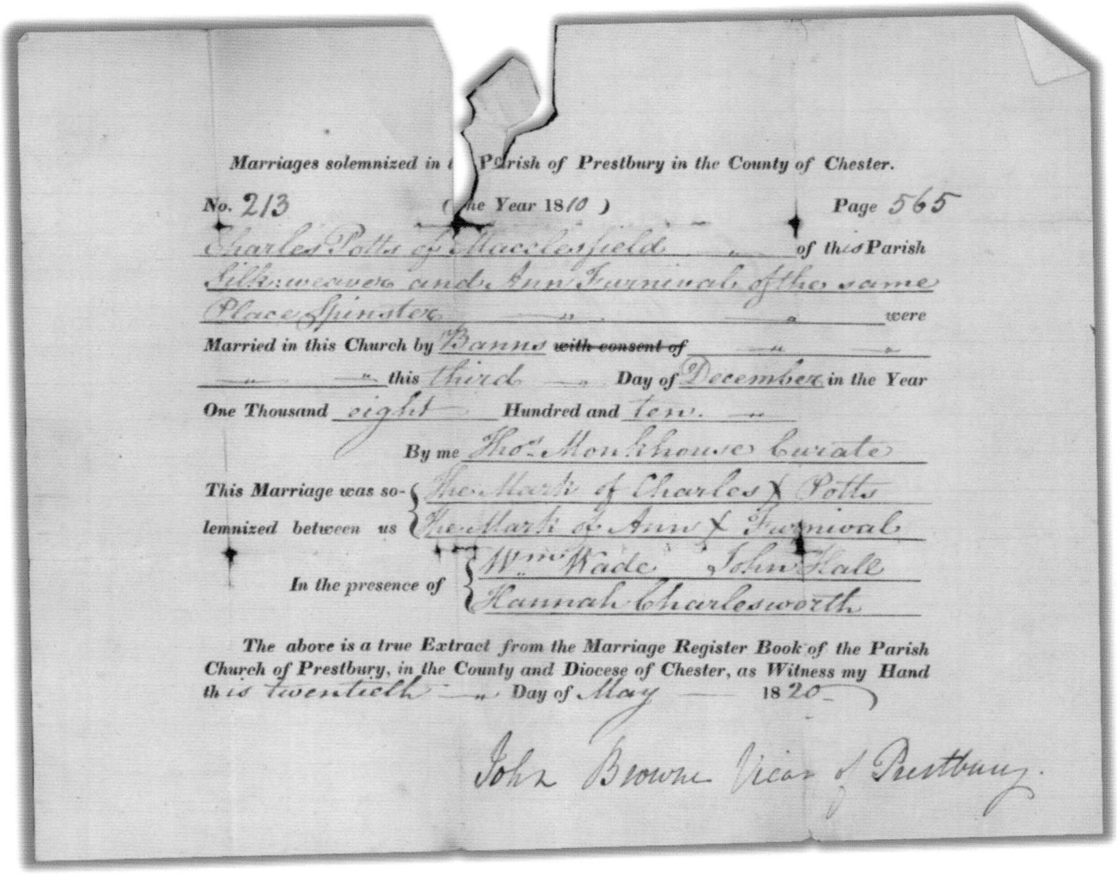

FIGURE 9-2: 1810 MARRIAGE CERTIFICATE OF CHARLES POTTS AND ANN FURNIVAL - EXTRACTED IN 1820

(IMAGE A052.156.002 FROM THE WIDECOMBE ARCHIVE)

The transcript of Figure 9-2 is as follows:

Marriages solemnized in [the] Parish of Prestbury in the County of Chester.
No. 213 the Year 1810 Page 565
Charles Potts of Macclesfield of this Parish
Silknweaver and Ann Furnival of the same
Place Spinster were
Married in this Church by Banns
this third Day of December in the Year
One Thousand eight Hundred and ten
By me Thos Monkhouse Curate
This Marriage was so-   {The Mark of Charles X Potts
lemnized between us   {The Mark of Ann X Furnival
*   {W^m Wade John Hale*
In the presence of   {Hannah Charlesworth
The above is a true Extract from the Marriage Register Book of the Parish
Church of Prestbury in the County and Diocese of Chester, as Witness my Hand
this twentieth Day of May 1820
John Brown Vicar of Prestbury

It seems that soon after the marriage Charles left Ann and moved to Plymouth where he married again without her knowledge (in Stoke Damerel Church to Maria Hannaford).

After a while he enlisted in the 22nd Foot Regiment and later died in service in 1820. Ann was left trying to fend for herself.

To uncover all these details (and this was in 1821 remember), there were examinations in Devon and Cheshire, as well as enquiries to verify the marriage in Prestbury, also in Cheshire, and also enquiries of the regiment concerned (see Figure 9-3, Figure 9-4, Figure 9-5 and Figure 9-7).

INTERESTING ASIDE 4: WIDECOMBE CHURCH

There has been a church at Widecombe since at least 1260 (see Bishop Bronscombe's Ordinacio - Chapter 13) and undoubtedly long before that.

The church was badly damaged in the Great Storm in October 1638 during divine service when ball lightning hit the tower and the roof causing numerous deaths and injuries from burning and falling masonry. Various contemporary accounts exist of this dreadful and unusual phenomenon.

The church was repaired after that disaster and by the period covered by this book must have been close to its current size and form, providing a good-sized space for the congregation.

Robert Dymond provides an interesting account of the architecture of the church and the story of the 1638 thunderstorm in his book "Things New and Old Concerning the Parish of Widecombe-in-the-Moor and Its Neighbourhood" published in 1876.

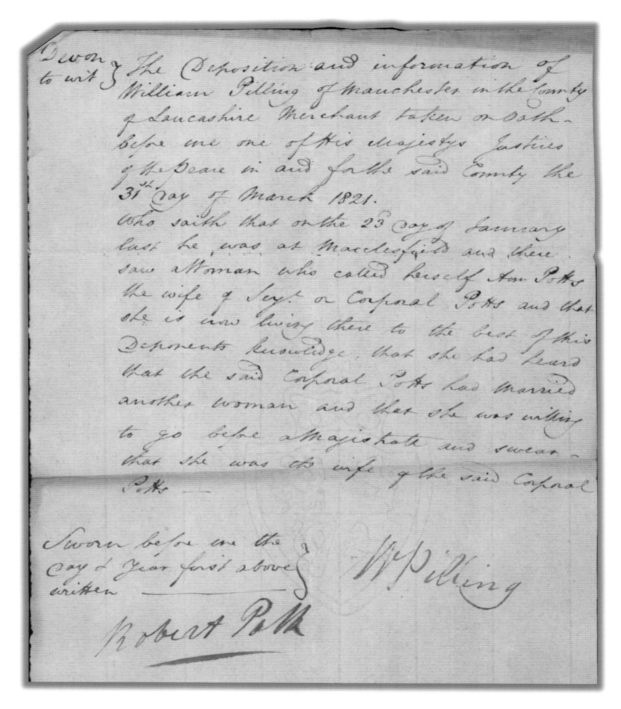

FIGURE 9-3: 1821 DEPOSITION OF ANN POTTS

(IMAGE A052.156.004 FROM THE WIDECOMBE ARCHIVE)

The transcript of Figure 9-3 is as follows:

Devon to wit
The Deposition and information of
William Pilling of Manchester in the County
of Lancashire Merchant taken on oath
before me one of this Majestys Justices
of the Peace in and for the said County the
31st day of March 1821
Who saith that on the 23d day of January
last he was at Macclesfield and there
saw a Woman who called herself Ann Potts
the wife of Sergt or Corporal Potts and that
she is now living there to the best of this
Deponents knowledge, that she had heard
that the said Corporal Potts had married
another Woman and that she was willing
to go before a Magistrate and swear
that she was the wife of the said Corporal
Potts
Sworn before me the   }
day of year first above   } W Pilling
written   }
Robert Palk

We then move on to information concerning Charles' second wife Maria, who was from Widecombe. She had an interesting life as shown in the two-page examination reproduced in Figure 9-4 and Figure 9-5:

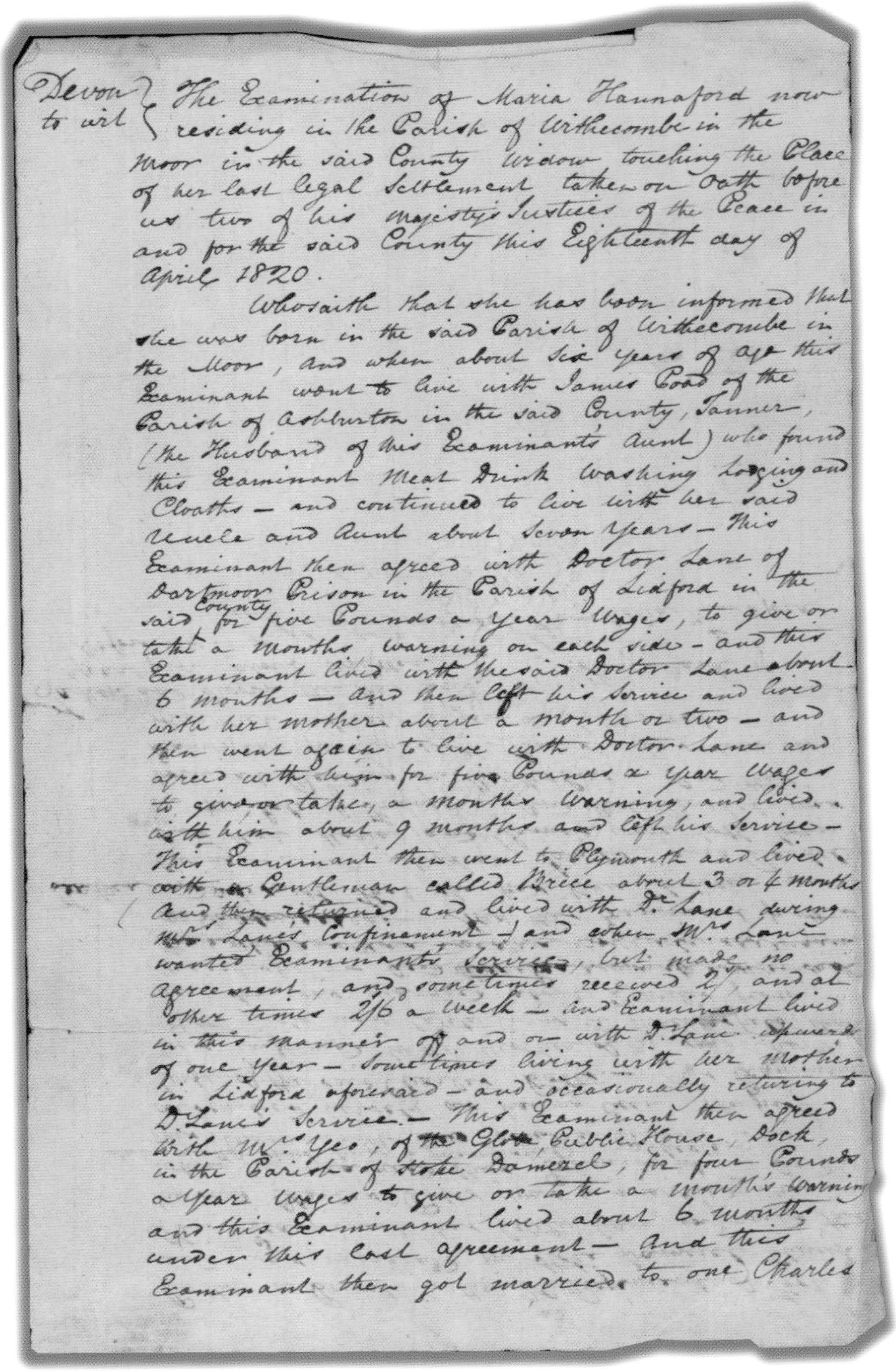

The transcript of Figure 9-4 is as follows:

Devon to wit
The Examination of Maria Hannaford now
residing in the Parish of Withecombe in the
Moor in the said County Widow touching the Place
of her last legal settlement taken on oath before
us two of his Majesty's Justices of the Peace in
and for the said County this Eighteenth day of
April 1820
Who saith that she has been informed that
she was born in the said Parish of Withecombe in
the Moor, and when about Six years of age this
Examinant went to live with James Poad of the
Parish of Ashburton in the said County, Tanner
(the Husband of this Examinants Aunt) who found
this Examinant Meat Drink Washing Lodging and
Cloaths - and continued to live with her said
Uncle and Aunt about seven years - This
Examinant then agreed with Doctor Lane of
Dartmoor Prison in the Parish of Lidford in the
said County for five Pounds a year Wages, to give or
take a months warning on each side - and this
Examinant lived with the said Doctor Lane about
6 months - and then left his Service and lived
with her mother about a Month or two - and
then went again to live with Doctor Lane and
agreed with him for five Pounds a year Wages
to give or take a Months warning, and lived-
with him about 9 months and left his service-
This Examinant then went to Plymouth and lived
with a Gentleman called Brice about 3 or 4 Months
And then returned and lived with Dr Lane during
Mrs Lanes Confinement - and when Mrs Lane
wanted Examinants service but made no
Agreement and sometimes received 2s, and at
other times 2/6 a Week - and Examinant lived
in this Manner off and on with Dr Lane upward
of one year - some times living with her mother
in Lidford aforesaid - and occasionally returning to
Dr Lanes service - this Examinant then agreed
With Mrs Yeo, of the Globe Public House Dock
in the Parish of Stoke Damerel for four Pounds
a year wages to give or take a months warning
and this Examinant lived about 6 months
under this last agreement - and this
Examinant then got married to one Charles

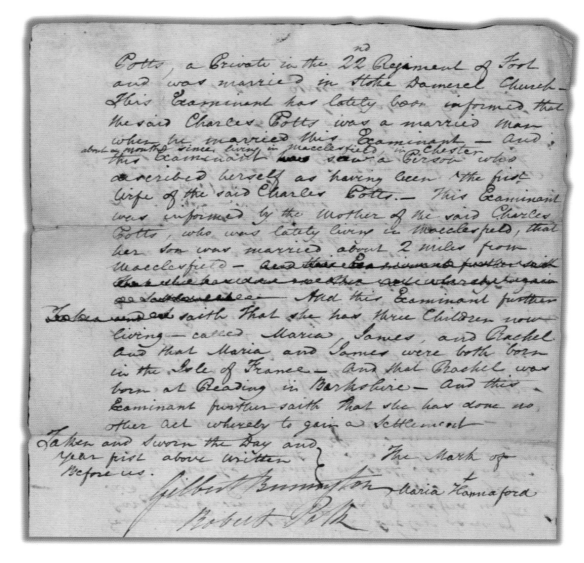

FIGURE 9-5: SECOND PAGE OF THE 1821 EXAMINATION OF MARIA HANNAFORD

(IMAGE A052.156.006.B FROM THE WIDECOMBE ARCHIVE)

The transcript of Figure 9-5 is as follows:

Potts a Private in the 22nd Regiment of Foot
and was married in Stoke Damerel Church
This Examinant has lately been informed that
the said Charles Potts was a married man
when he married this Examinant - And
about a month since living in Macclesfield, in Chester
this Examinant saw a Person who
described herself as having been the first
Wife of the said Charles Potts- This Examinant
was informed by the Mother of the said Charles
Potts, who was lately living in Macclesfield, that
her son was married about 2 miles from
Macclesfield - And this Examinant further
saith that she has three Children now

*living called Maria, James, and Rachel
and that Maria and James were both born
in the Isle of France - And that Rachel was
born at Reading in Barkshire- And this
Examinant further saith that she has done no
other Act whereby to gain a Settlement*

Taken and Sworn the Day and   *} The Mark of*
year first above written   *}*   *+*
Before us.   *} Maria Hannaford*
Gilbert Burrington
Robert Palk

We also find that Maria Hannaford and her children are being supported in Widecombe in 1821 which explains the investigation into her true place of settlement. Figure 9-6 shows a payment of £1 12s to her family, one of several regular amounts paid at that time.

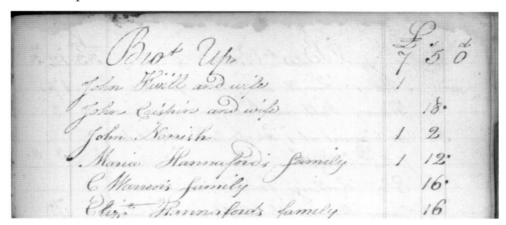

FIGURE 9-6: DETAIL FROM THE OVERSEERS' ACCOUNTS FOR 1821 SHOWING PAYMENT TO MARIA HANNAFORD'S FAMILY

(IMAGE A007.011.P021 FROM THE WIDECOMBE ARCHIVE)

Maria was examined again in September 1821[65], but perhaps not surprisingly the content of the examination appears almost identical. The matter was complicated by the death of Charles Potts as shown in the letter from the War Office in 1820 (Figure 9-7 below). Note that it does not say how he died.

---

[65] See A052.038 in the Widecombe Archive

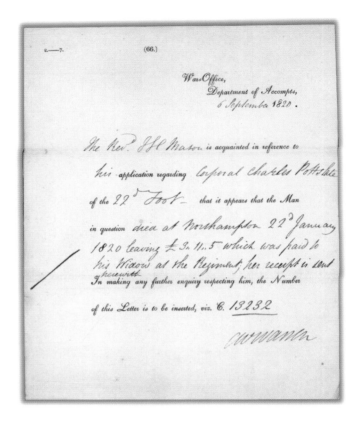

FIGURE 9-7: LETTER FROM THE WAR OFFICE CONFIRMING CHARLES POTTS' DEATH

(IMAGE A052.156.007 FROM THE WIDECOMBE ARCHIVE)

The transcript of Figure 9-7 is as follows:

War=Office,
Department of Accompts,
6 September 1820.
The Rev^d JH Mason is acquainted in reference to
his application regarding Corporal Charles Potts late
of the 22^d Foot that it appears that the Man
in question died at Northampton 22^d January
1820 leaving £3 11 5 which was paid to
his Widow at the Regiment, her receipt is sent
herewith
In making any further enquiry respecting him the Number
of this Letter is to be inserted, viz C. 13232
CW Warren

There is no Removal Order in the records that have survived. This may mean that no decision was taken to remove Maria. However, by 1822 she disappears from the record, although there are entries for 'Maria Hawkin's family' instead, which may or may not be connected. Did she change or name? Did she marry? If she did it does not appear to have altered her circumstances.

The image in Figure 9-8 shows the Justice of the Peace, Robert Palk's, approval of payments to the poor including Maria Hannaford: £3 1s 12d already paid and £1 8s 'intend to pay'.

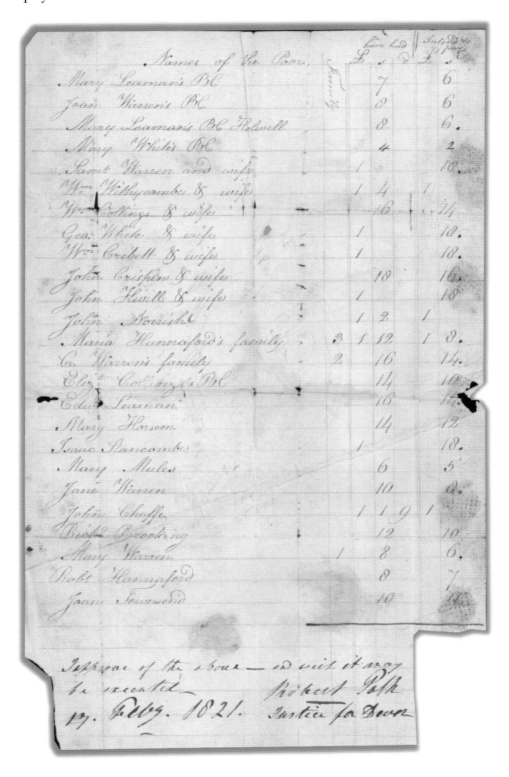

FIGURE 9-8: SHEET LISTING ROBERT PALK'S APPROVAL OF PAYMENTS TO THE POOR OF WIDECOMBE DATED FEBRUARY 1821 INCLUDING MARIA HANNAFORD'S FAMILY

(IMAGE A052.392.F FROM THE WIDECOMBE ARCHIVE)

The expenses of such investigations were considerable, involving time and, sometimes, long-distance travel (as in this case). An idea of the costs of some of the proceedings that were necessary to pursue the law and ensure that Overseers only paid out what was right under that law is shown in Figure 9-9, where £29 8s 7d was paid for the costs on appeal of a case before the Queen's Bench. Sadly, we don't appear to have any details of this case, although no doubt the Queen's Bench has records.

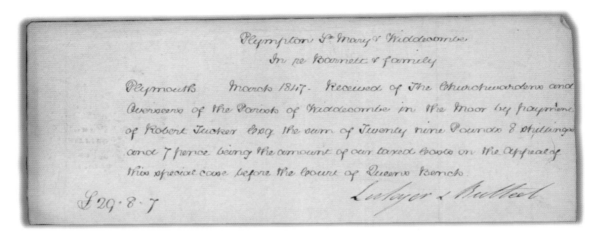

FIGURE 9-9: SHEET LISTING EXPENSES FOR DEALING WITH THE CASE OF BARNETT AND FAMILY IN 1847

(IMAGE A052.153.F FROM THE WIDECOMBE ARCHIVE)

The transcript of Figure 9-9 is as follows:

Plympton St Mary & Widdecombe
In re Barnett & family
Plymouth March 1847 Received of The Churchwardens and
Overseers of the Parish of Widdecombe in the Moor by payment
of Robert Tucker Esq the sum of Twenty nine Pounds 8 shillings
and 7 pence being the amount of our taxed Costs on the Appeal of
this special case before the Court of Queens Bench
Lockyer & Butler & C
£29 - 8 - 7

The Robert Tucker mentioned here is almost certainly the Ashburton solicitor, who crops up very frequently in Widecombe documents.

A PARISH OFFICER's JOURNAL!!

ROSE early, and reflected on the dignity of my office—put on my beſt wig, to create awe and reverence in my family—Betty my wife's new maid ſervant not ſufficiently ſtruck by my appearance—a great deal too free—remember to give her warning— ate a hearty breakfaſt and looked over the pariſh accounts—Tom Giles, the Painter, charges too much for mending the commandments—remember not to employ him about John the Baptiſt's head in the charger—add a few pounds to the repairing of the pulpit and reading deſk, and ſpeculate on the gallery windows—remember to have my name placed in a conſpicuous ſituation, facing the middle aiſle—put on my beſt clothes, and ſet out to meet the gentlemen of the annoyance jury—met Bill Jenkins, the Glazier—paſſed by me without touching his hat—call on him for his arrears of the window tax—ſet out with the jury from the veſtry room at eleven o'clock preciſely— a moſt awful and ſublime appearance—remember to get the beadles larger hats—they want weight and dignity—overſet ſix old women's apple barrows, and brought off the property—chaffed the light weights and meaſures with infinite ſucceſs—dined with the gentlemen at the Cat and Bag Pipes—returned home ſoon in order to prepare for the evening's entertainment—ſeveral applications from the poor—impoſſible to pay attention to every thing—took my afternoon's nap—dreamt about fees of office—looked over my little perquiſites, and adjuſted my wig—had half an hours bickering with my wife to keep up my conſequence—and ſet out to meet my pariſh friends at the George, where we made a moſt excellent ſupper, on the profits of a *child*, and adjuſted ſeveral weighty parochial concerns, while partaking of the good things the landlord prepared for us, which conſiſted of rumps of beef, legs of mutton, ſuet puddings, fat geeſe, onions, and other light and delicate articles—ſpent the evening very convivially, and made up another party for the day enſuing.

PRINTED BY E. SPRAGG. 27. BOW-STREET, COVENT-GARDEN.

FIGURE 9-10: THOMAS ROWLANDSON (1757-1827): A PARISH OFFICER'S JOURNAL. 1802

(THE ELISHA WHITTELSEY COLLECTION, METROPOLITAN MUSEUM OF ART, PUBLIC DOMAIN)

THE CASE OF GEORGE LEAMAN, HIS WIFE AND THREE CHILDREN

On 15th June 1843 an order was made to the Churchwardens and Overseers of Widecombe and Lidford that George and his family be removed from Widecombe to Lidford and for the Churchwardens and Overseers of Lidford to 'receive and provide for' them (Figure 9-11).

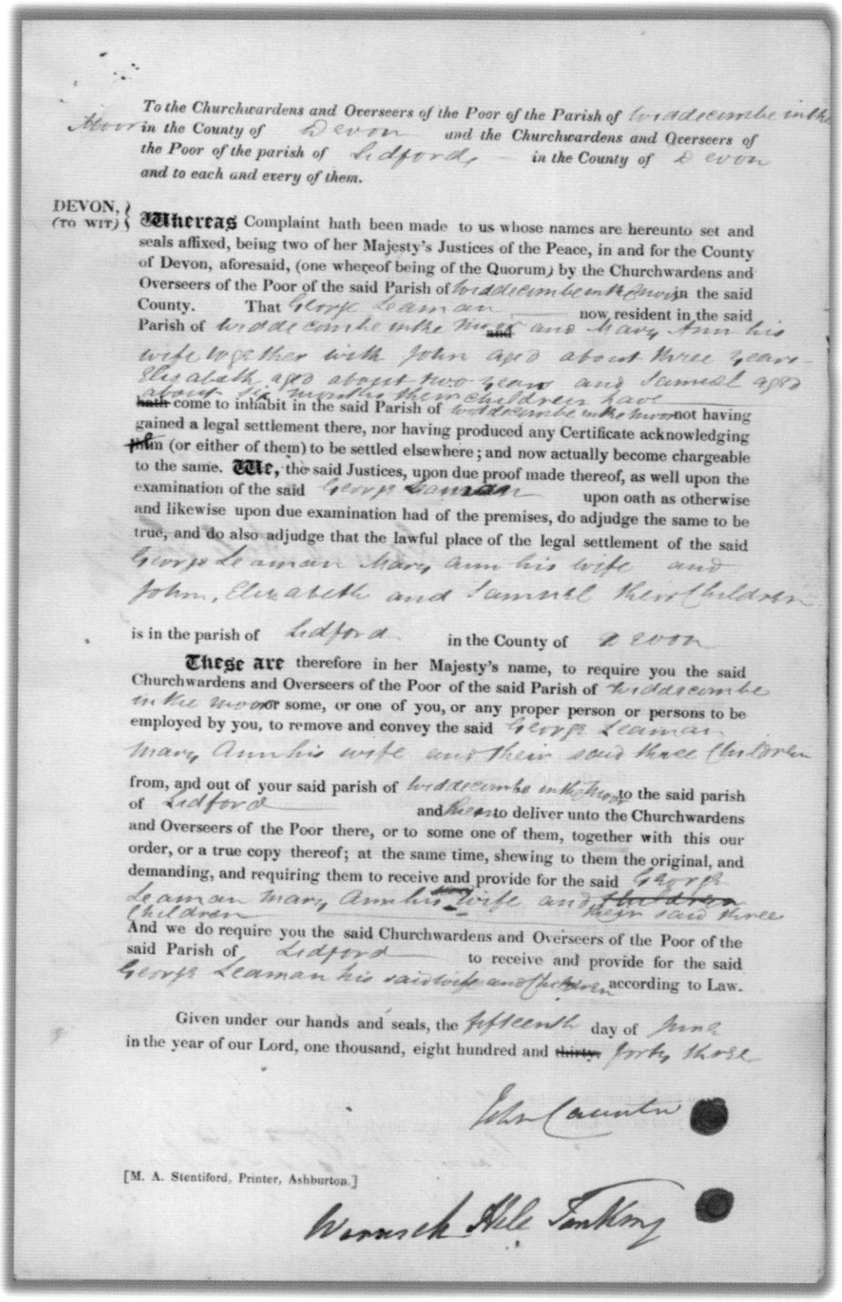

FIGURE 9-11: 1843 REMOVAL ORDER FOR GEORGE LEAMAN AND FAMILY

(IMAGE A052.021.003.F FROM THE WIDECOMBE ARCHIVE)

The transcript of Figure 9-11 is as follows:

To the Churchwardens and Overseers of the Poor of the Parish of Widdecombe in the
Moor in the County of Devon and the Churchwardens and Overseers of
the Poor of the parish of Lidford in the County of Devon
and to each and every of them.
DEVON, (TO WIT)
Whereas complaint hath been made to us whose names are hereunto set and
seals affixed, being two of her Majesty's Justices of the Peace, in and for the County
of Devon, aforesaid, (one whereof being of the Quorum) by the Churchwardens and
Overseers of the Poor of the said Parish of Widdecombe in the Moor in the said
County. That George Leaman now resident in the said
Parish of Widdecombe in the Moor and Mary Ann his
wife together with John aged about three years
Elizabeth aged about two years and Samuel aged
about six months their children have
come to inhabit in the said Parish of Widdecombe in the Moor not having
gained a legal settlement there, nor having produced any Certificate acknowledging
them (or either of them) to be settled elsewhere; and now actually become
chargeable
to the same. We the said Justices, upon due proof made thereof, as well upon the
examination of the said George Leaman upon oath as otherwise
and likewise upon due examination had of the premises, do adjudge the same to be
true, and do also adjudge that the lawful place of the legal settlement of the said
George Leaman Mary Ann his wife and
John, Elizabeth and Samuel their Children
is in the parish of Lidford in the County of Devon
These are therefore in her Majesty's name, to require you the said
Churchwardens and Overseers of the Poor of the said Parish of Widdecombe
in the Moor or some, or one of you, or any proper person or persons to be
employed by you, to remove and convey the said George Leaman
Mary Ann his wife and their said three Children
from, and out of your said parish of Widdecombe in the Moor to the said parish
of Lidford and them to deliver unto the Churchwardens
and Overseers of the Poor there, or to some one of them, together with this our
order, or a true copy thereof; at the same time, shewing to them the original and
demanding, and requiring them to receive and provide for the said George
Leaman Mary Ann his wife and their said three Children
And we do require you the said Churchwardens and Overseers of the Poor of the
said Parish of Lidford to receive and provide for the said
George Leaman his said wife and Children according to Law.
Given under our hands and seals, the fifteenth day of June
in the year of our Lord, one thousand eight hundred and forty three
John Caunter
Warwick Hele Tonkin

[M. A. Stentiford, Printer, Ashburton.]

On 16th June 1843 another Removal Order was issued to remove George Leaman, his wife and young family to Lidford from Widecombe (see Figure 9-12).

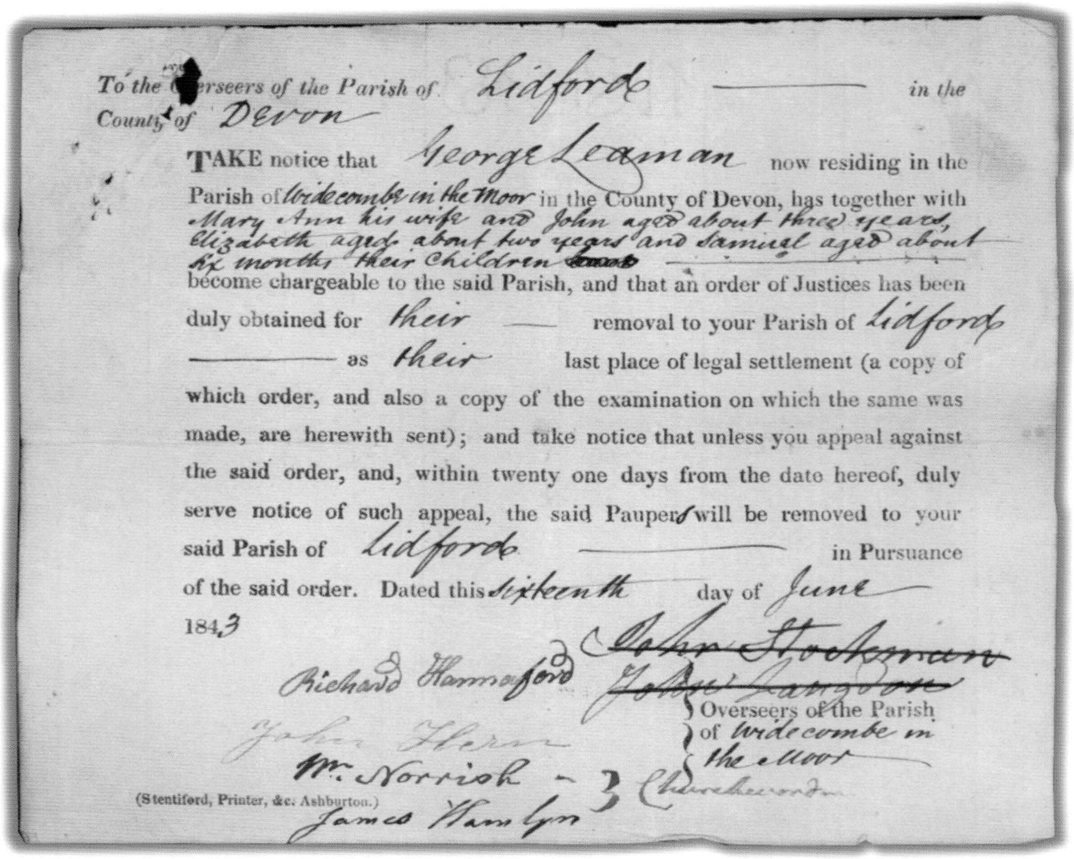

FIGURE 9-12: SECOND 1843 REMOVAL ORDER FOR GEORGE LEAMAN AND FAMILY

(IMAGE A052.021.001 FROM THE WIDECOMBE ARCHIVE)

The transcript of Figure 9-12 is as follows:

To the Overseers of the Parish of Lidford in the
County of Devon
TAKE notice that George Leaman now residing in the
Parish of Widecombe in the Moor in the County of Devon, has together with
Mary Ann his wife and John aged about three years
Elizabeth aged about two years and Samuel aged about
six months their children
become chargeable to the said Parish, and that an order of Justices has been
duly obtained for their removal to your Parish of Lidford
as their last place of legal settlement (a copy of
which order, and also a copy of the examination on which the same was
made, are herewith sent): and take notice that unless you appeal against
the said order, and, within twenty one days from the date hereof, duly
serve notice of such appeal, the said Paupers will be removed to your
said Parish of Lidford in Pursuance

of the said order. Dated this sixteenth day of June
1843
Richard Hannaford } Overseers of the Parish
John Hern   } of Widecombe in
                    } the Moor

Wm Norrish   }
James Hamlyn   } Churchwarden

(Stentiford, Printer, &c. Ashburton.)

The removal had been suspended the day before because George was unable to travel 'by reason of sickness and infirmity'. We know from later testimonies that this is because he had a broken leg, which must have been a major problem for him and rendering him unable to work. It also appears that this broken leg is the reason he is being removed in the first place. If he didn't have the injury he wouldn't be seeking relief and therefore there would be no reason to have him removed.

The examinations go on to investigate George's parents (John and Gertrude) whose home parish was Lidford. From 1839, Lidford paid for the family to remain in Widecombe rather than send them to the poor house at Tavistock. (Note that this was in the time of the Unions - see Chapter 10 on Newton Abbot Union - and Lidford was within the Tavistock Union, just as Widecombe was within the Newton Abbot Union).

The documents show that on 26 March 1839, John Leaman, his wife Gertrude and daughter were ordered to be removed to Lidford and this order was never appealed against. The family was handed over to a John Hamlin at Two Bridges. In May of that year Thomas Hannaford was paid the maintenance costs covering March - May 1839 from the same John Hamlin. This suggests that the family came straight back, and indeed Gertrude's testimony suggests that they came back and lived in Widecombe.

George worked for his father as a thatcher for a while, but by the time of the 1843 investigations John is a 'bed-lier', i.e. presumably bedridden and therefore unable to work and fend for himself and this has probably been the case since at least 1839 and may be why he was removed at that time.

From George's testimony it looks as if the family lived at Widecombe throughout George's life (and he was twenty-six in 1843) and in 1843 because of George's incapacity, the Overseers are taking advantage of the 'lack of legal settlement' of George in Widecombe to have him and his family removed back to Lidford, despite them never having lived there (although it is true that Lidford is his place of settlement because that is his parents place of settlement). He also married his wife Mary Ann in 1839 in Widecombe Church. Quite where they would go in Lidford and what they would do would appear to be something of a mystery. Presumably it would have to be the workhouse for the entire family if George had no means to support them in any other way.

We don't yet know how this story ends (perhaps the records of the Tavistock Union will help here) but it could be clearly investigated further. It illustrates the problems that can arise if you fell ill in those days and were away from your place of legal settlement. You would suddenly lose any security you felt you might have.

MARY HAMLYN AND HER SIX CHILDREN

Finally, we will examine the case of Mary Hamlyn together with her six children. Mary was living in Stoke Damerel in 1857 with her six children, who were aged between two and fourteen. She was married to John Hamlyn but he was 'absent from her'. John is 'legally settled' in Widecombe and therefore Mary and her children should be settled there.

A Removal Order was raised by Devonport (on behalf of Stoke Damerel) against Widecombe. The basis of the settlement ruling was that John was apprenticed to William Mann at Cator and he stayed there throughout the period of his apprenticeship. This was appealed by Widecombe, which basically means that they did not agree with the basis of the Order. Although the handwriting in this case is extremely difficult to interpret (a problem that has been found only rarely during research), it appears that the grounds for the appeal were that Cator was not in Widecombe parish but was in Lydford parish. In fact this is not true; the various Cator settlements are all in Widecombe. Some of them are close to the boundary with the old 'Forest Quarter' it is true (which Quarter reverted to Lydford in 1818 or so), but they have never been actually in that Quarter and any claim that they were in Lydford is erroneous. A letter from Devonport actually makes the same point, but even so, soon afterwards the removal order was abandoned. If the reader would like to investigate this case in more detail, try searching in the Widecombe Archive for A052.386a and A052.386a2.

CHAPTER 10 NEWTON ABBOT UNION

The major overhaul to the Poor Law system that followed on from the Royal Commission in 1832 - the Poor Law Amendment Act of 1834 (see Chapter 2 'Background and Context'), meant that the administration of the Poor Law system changed substantially to a more regionally based system from a local parish-based system. This was achieved through the joining together of a number of parishes into a 'union' or grouping. In Widecombe's case this meant joining the newly-formed 'Newton Abbot Union' (NAU), which although still recognising and involving the parishes, would have as its centrepiece the newly built Newton Abbot Union Workhouse constructed on East Street.

FIGURE 10-1: FRONT PAGE OF THE ORDER FOR THE FORMATION OF THE NEWTON ABBOT UNION IN 1836 (CATALOGUE ITEM (PLU/GEN/8/3 FROM THE SW HERITAGE TRUST DEVON ARCHIVES)

"Newton Abbot Poor Law Union was formed on 20th June 1836 and the workhouse was built in 1837 in East Street, Newton Abbot. In 1878 the workhouse had room for about 400 inmates. The wards, yards etc. occupied 2 acres and there were gardens adjoining. Newton Dispensary was established in 1858 and the Cottage Hospital opened in East Street, Newton Abbot in 1873. The hospital belonged to the trustees in fee and was managed by 'a committee of ladies and gentlemen of the town'. It was supported by voluntary contributions, annual subscriptions and patient fees. The Newton Cottage Hospital and Dispensary was later known as Newton Abbot Hospital and Dispensary. The workhouse became the Newton Abbot Public Assistance Institution and the buildings later formed part of Newton Abbot Hospital".[66]

Figure 10-1 shows the front page of the Order for the formation of the Union. This document goes on to list the requirements that need to be fulfilled and, by a separate document, the records that need to be kept. Note that Figure 10-1 also shows the parishes that were included in the Union, which include Widecombe, Manaton, Moreton Hampstead, Buckland in the Moor as well as lowland areas such as Cockington and Torbryan.

The 1832 Commission had recommended in its report that workhouses be separated according to class of resident, i.e. by age, and sex, and health, leading to at least 4 separate groupings.[67] And this was to be in separate institutions, not just in different parts of the same building. However, the system was never implemented that way and the new Union at Newton Abbot, for example, was a single large establishment. According to Webb,[68] there was never an explanation as to why the law was implemented in this way, although there was reference to the advantages of 'one strong, efficient building'[69]. The 'General Mixed Workhouse', as it was called, was, of course, the way that the system had operated at the Church House in Widecombe. There was, no doubt, some segregation, but this was probably very limited by the size of the building and the wide range of people that had to be accommodated, from the old and infirm, those that were sick and/or bedridden, to young mothers with babies or about to give birth, right through to young children. You can imagine the range of people that might have been residing in the Church House at different times and this did not change with the Union arrangement. It was not just a testing place for the able-bodied man and his wife and dependent children but, in the Commissioners own words 'likewise a receptacle for the sick, the aged and bedridden, deserted children and vagrants, as well as harmless idiots: classes of

---

[66] From SW Heritage Trust (cat ref 6223A).

[67] See Webb 1929, page 122.

[68] Ibid., page 123.

[69] Ibid., page 127.

persons who need constant and careful supervision. It includes a nursery, a school, an infirmary and a place of temporary confinement'.[70]

FIGURE 10-2: INMATES AND STAFF OUTSIDE UNION HOUSE IN EAST STREET GATHERED FOR THE PARADE TO MARK THE DIAMOND JUBILEE OF QUEEN VICTORIA IN JUNE 1897

(IMAGE FROM A PRIVATE COLLECTION - USED WITH PERMISSION)

Once the NAU was formed, the Overseers of the Poor were no longer as involved in the day-to-day work of looking after the Poor. This responsibility transferred to the Guardians of the Poor as part of the amalgamation or 'union' of parish poor relief. (However, Overseers still existed and were probably still involved in assessment and money payments etc. - as testified by documents that continue to be addressed to them).

Also, it was not intended that Newton Abbot Workhouse should necessarily replace existing local provision (at least initially - but see Chapter 7 for an attempt to keep the Church House going), so the use of the Church House as a workhouse continued. In effect it was the administration that had changed, so rather than the Overseers being responsible for collecting the Poor Rate and for dispensing the relief

---

[70] Webb 1929, page 127.

to the poor this now transferred to the Union, although it looks as if the dispensation continued to be made locally with the money being provided by the Union.

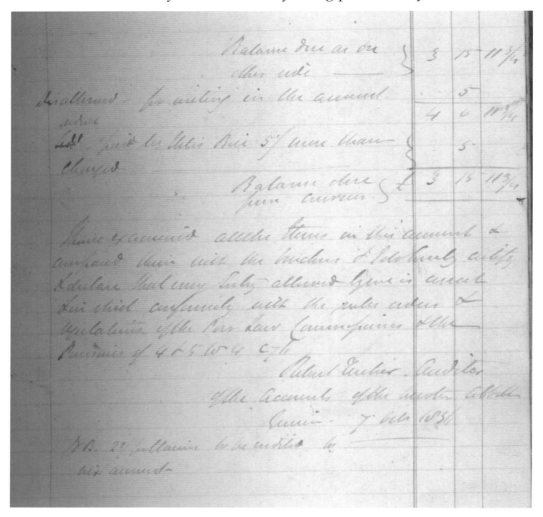

FIGURE 10-3: PAGE FROM THE 1836 OVERSEERS' ACCOUNTS

(IMAGE A031.P103 FROM THE WIDECOMBE ARCHIVE)

Figure 10-3 shows the final Widecombe Overseers' Accounts being taken over by the Newton Abbot Union in 1836.

A partial transcription of the extract in Figure 10-3 follows (although the writing is quite hard to decipher):

I have examined all the Items in this Account &
compared them with the vouchers & I do hereby certify
& declare that [..]
& in strict conformity with the rules orders
regulations of the Poor Law Commissioners…

Thereafter, the Poor Rate collection was a Newton Abbot Union responsibility. There is a rate book for 1847 showing the collection of this rate for the fourth quarter, or the fourth assessment for the year 1847-1848.

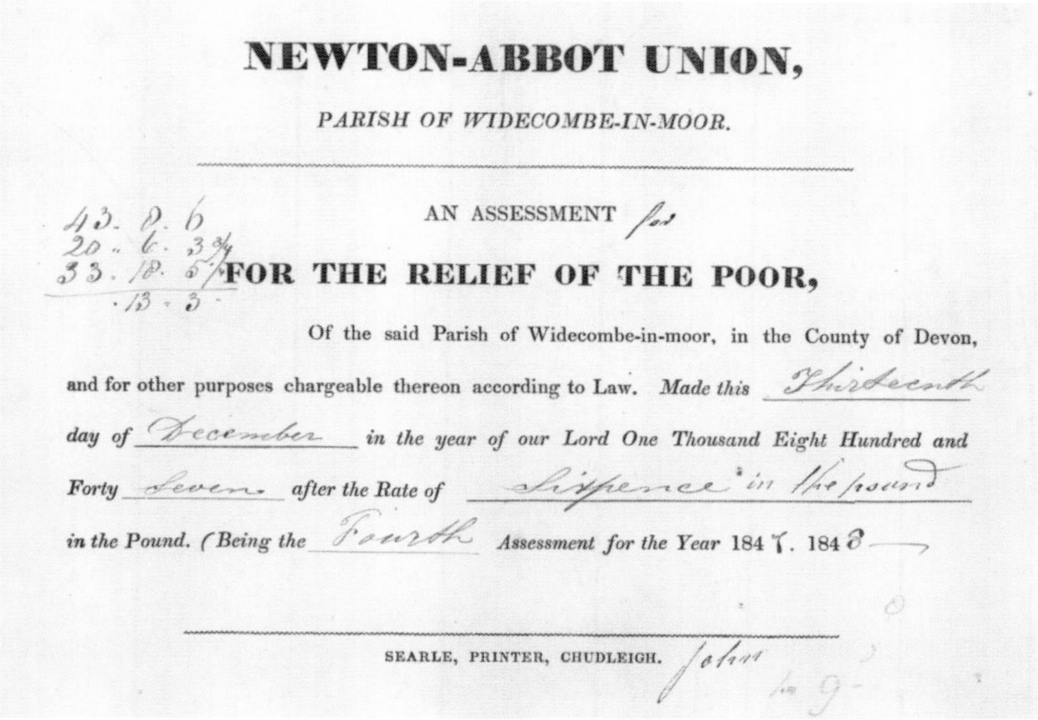

NEWTON-ABBOT UNION,

PARISH OF WIDECOMBE-IN-MOOR.

AN ASSESSMENT for

FOR THE RELIEF OF THE POOR,

Of the said Parish of Widecombe-in-moor, in the County of Devon, and for other purposes chargeable thereon according to Law. *Made this* Thirteenth *day of* December *in the year of our Lord One Thousand Eight Hundred and Forty* Seven *after the Rate of* Sixpence in the pound *in the Pound. (Being the* Fourth *Assessment for the Year* 1847. 1848

SEARLE, PRINTER, CHUDLEIGH.

FIGURE 10-4: FRONT PAGE FROM THE 1847 POOR RATE BOOK

(IMAGE H251.P001 FROM THE WIDECOMBE ARCHIVE)

The first page of this rate book is shown in Figure 10-5 and Figure 10-6 to illustrate the amounts payable by the landowners and occupiers. Note the column entitled 'No of Votes'. This was because the landowners or occupiers had a number of votes that was calculated based on the rateable value of their land when appointing the local representative to the Guardians of the Poor. It appears from the formation documents that Widecombe was eligible to have one Guardian appointed.

Note entry number 10 in this list. It is for Samuel Taylor Coldridge[71] as the Occupier with the Dean and Chapter of Exeter as the owner and the property concerned is the Great Tithes for the Parish of Widecombe. Mr Coldridge had leased the tithes from the Dean and Chapter and so received the regular payments of tithes in exchange. From the right-hand sheet it can be seen that the rateable value of this tithe was £123 15s, considerably higher than any other property and that as a result he paid £3 1s 10½d as his contribution to the Poor Rate. So, the recipient of the Great Tithes income was assessed for rates on those tithes, including the Poor Rate.

Accounts show County and Police Rate being paid out of the Poor Rate. It was clearly the ancestor of the system of 'rates' (now known as 'council tax') that property owners and occupiers pay today.

[71] No relation to the well-known poet, as far as we know and whose name is, of course, spelt slightly differently.

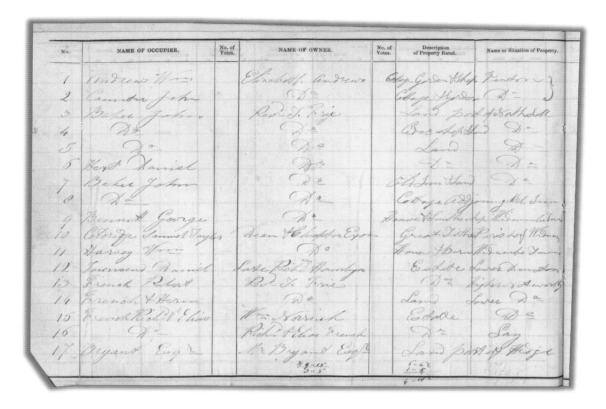

FIGURE 10-5: FRONT PAGE (LEFT-HAND-SIDE) FROM THE 1847 POOR RATE BOOK
(IMAGE H251.P002 FROM THE WIDECOMBE ARCHIVE)

FIGURE 10-6: FRONT PAGE (RIGHT-HAND-SIDE) FROM THE 1847 POOR RATE BOOK
(IMAGE H251.P003 FROM THE WIDECOMBE ARCHIVE)

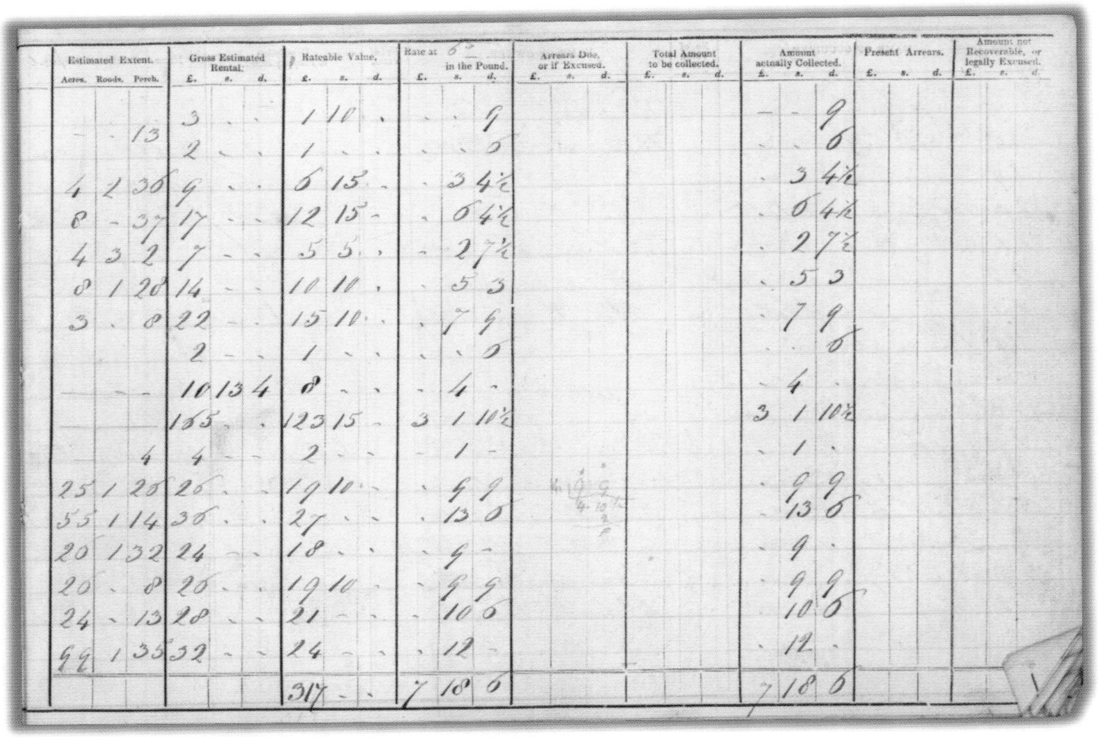

Document H257 in the Widecombe Archive shows the Newton Abbot Union Financial and Statistical Statement for the half-year ended Michaelmas 1852. Details are provided for each parish in the Union. The entries are interesting as they highlight the financial transactions that were involved in the running of each Parish. The entry for Widecombe reads as follows:

Area in Acres	11300
Population (from the 1851 Census)	974
Balance in favour at the start	£40 2s 9d
Receipts	
Contributions Received	£177 0s 0d
Balances, disallowances etc paid to the treasurer	£16 1s 4d
Relief transferred to common fund	
Pensions relief repaid etc	
From paymaster of Civil Service	
Balance against parish at the end of the half-year	
Total	£233 4s 1d
Expenses	
In maintenance	£12 10s 9½d
Out-relief in money and in kind including to non-resident poor	£126 0s 8d
Relief by way of loan	
Maintenance of lunatics in Asylums or Licensed Houses	
Extra medical fees	£3 0s 0d
Emigration expenses	
Vaccination fees	
Registration fees	£1 12s 6d
County Rates	£27 17s 11d
Expenses of receiving pensions, rent of room to pay poor and sundries	
Relief transferred	
Workhouse loan and interest repaid	£10 3s 3 d
Salaries	£30 3s 6 d
Balance in favour at half-year end	£21 15s 7d
Total	£233 4s 1d
Average of separate expenditure for the relief of the poor:	
Three years before the formation of the Union	£474
three years ended lady-day 1850	£261

It is interesting to see the amount of money paid as out-relief (the majority) suggesting that the money was paid to Widecombe and dispensed locally. This document also shows that the County Rate continued to be collected and paid out this way, as previously.

On the reverse side of the 1852 Financial Statement is the Statistical Statement. Here are listed the various paupers by type that received relief in the half-year. The Widecombe entry reads as follows:

In-door

- Adult Able-bodied 'Other Female' - 1
- Adult Not Able-bodied 'Other Male' - 5
- Adult Not Able-bodied 'Other Female' - 2
- Orphans or other children relieved without parents - 3

Out-door

able-bodied

- Adult Males relieved in cases of their own Accident, Illness or Infirmity - 9
- Adult Males relieved in cases of Accident, Illness or Infirmity of family or a funeral - 4
- Families of the above adult males resident with their father - Wife - 5
- Families of the above adult males resident with their father - Children under 16 - 14
- Widows - 7
- Children under 16 dependant upon widows - 17
- Single women without children - 3
- Illegitimate children and their mothers - mothers - 1 children - 1

Non able-bodied

- Male - 20
- Female - 43
- Children under 16 relieved with parents - 3
- Orphaned or other children under 16 relieved without parents - 5
- Lunatics, insane persons and idiots Male - 4

Female - 1

Some of these figures are particularly enlightening. For instance, twenty males and forty-three females who are not able-bodied (although this may, of course, have been temporary disablement - the statement is not clear on this point. It could also have reflected the elderly). Also, there are four males and one female who are considered lunatic or otherwise insane or mentally diminished in some way.

We can also see from a much later Widecombe parish statement (1894) that payments were due from the parish of Widecombe for the poor of Widecombe. So, although the administration was more centralised, the parish still paid according to the relief required within their own parish and did not pay a general rate across all the parishes. The numbers were also considerably down compared to earlier times. Perhaps this was a result of the increased centralisation of the poor relief system? Perhaps families were now more responsible for their own members?

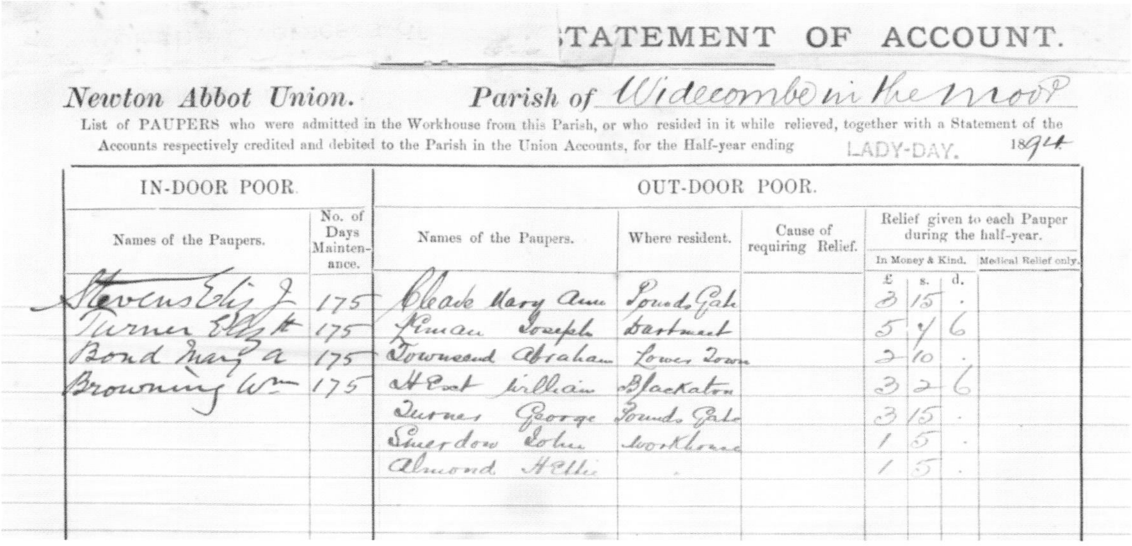

FIGURE 10-7: DETAIL FROM THE HALF-YEAR ENDING LADY DAY 1894 STATEMENT OF ACCOUNT OF NEWTON ABBOT UNION FOR THE PARISH OF WIDECOMBE

(IMAGE A046.023.P001 FROM THE WIDECOMBE ARCHIVE)

A partial transcript of Figure 10-7 is shown below.

[S]TATEMENT OF ACCOUNT.
Newton Abbot Union. Parish of Widecombe in the Moor
List of PAUPERS who were admitted in the Workhouse from this Parish, or who resided in it while relieved, together with a Statement of the Accounts respectively credited and debited to the Parish in the Union Accounts, for the Half-year ending LADY-DAY 1894.

IN-DOOR POOR.

Names of the Paupers.	No. of Days Maintenance.
Stevens Eliz J	175
Turner Eliz^th	175
Bond Mary A	175
Browning W^m	175

OUT-DOOR POOR.
Relief given to each Pauper during the half-year.

Names of the Paupers.	Where resident.	Cause of requiring Relief.	In Money & Kind.	Medical Relief only.
Cleave Mary Ann	Pounds Gate		£3 15s 0	
Leman Joseph	Dartmeet		£5 7s 6d	
Townsend Abraham	Lower Town		£2 10s 0d	
Hext William	Blackaton		£3 2s 6d	
Turner George	Pounds Gate		£3 15s 0d	
Smerdon John	Workhouse		£1 5s 0d	
Almond Hettie	"		£1 5s 0d	

Note that there were some in-house poor, which presumably means that there were some poor from Widecombe who were located in the workhouse at Newton Abbot. Also mentioned are John Smerdon and Hettie Almond who were out-door poor but their address is given as 'Workhouse', which presumably means they were in the Church House Widecombe.

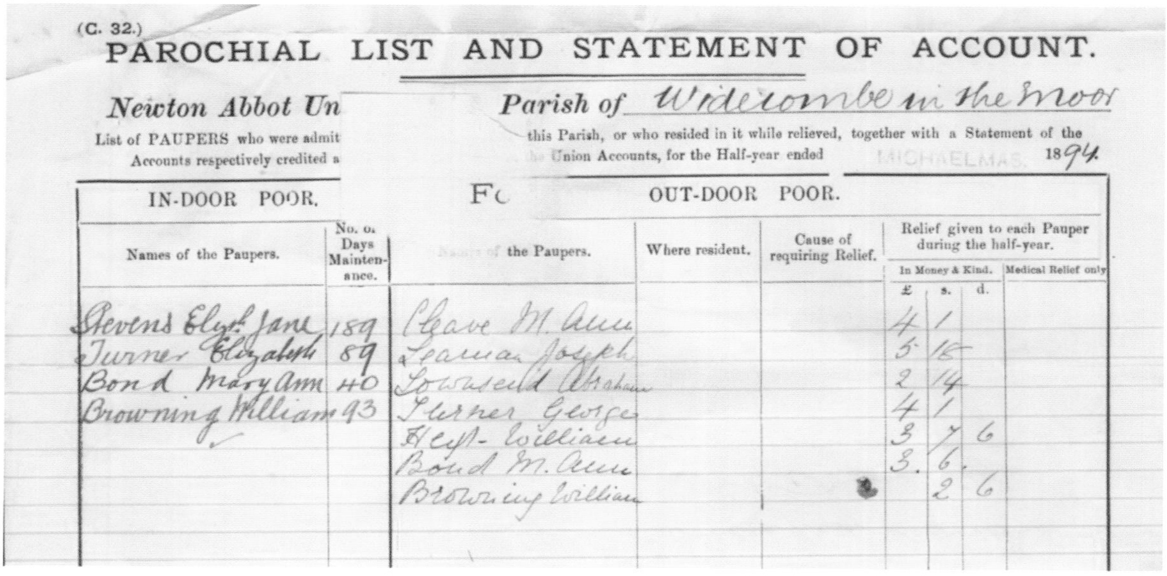

FIGURE 10-8: DETAIL FROM THE HALF-YEAR ENDING MICHAELMAS 1894 STATEMENT OF ACCOUNT OF NEWTON ABBOT UNION FOR THE PARISH OF WIDECOMBE

(IMAGE A046.024.P001 FROM THE WIDECOMBE ARCHIVE)

A partial transcript of Figure 10-8 is given below and shows the differences between the first and second half-years of 1894. The same four people are in the workhouse at Newton Abbot, but two of them leave during the second half-year and become receivers of outdoor relief but we do not know where they are residing as that column is not completed.

IN-DOOR POOR.

Names of the Paupers.	No. of Days Maintenance.
Stevens Elizth Jane	189
Turner Elizabeth	89
Bond Mary Ann	40
Browning William	43

OUT-DOOR POOR.

Names of the Paupers.	Where resident.	Cause of requiring Relief.	In Money & Kind.	Medical Relief only.
Cleave M Ann			£4 1s 0d	
Leman Joseph			£5 18s 0d	
Townsend Abraham			£2 14s 0d	
Turner George			£4 1s 0d	
Hext William			£3 7s 6d	
Bond M Ann			£3 6s 0d	
Browning William			£0 2s 6d	

Finally, we can look at the following half-year to Lady Day 1895 as shown by Figure 10-9. The date is omitted but we can derive it from other documents.

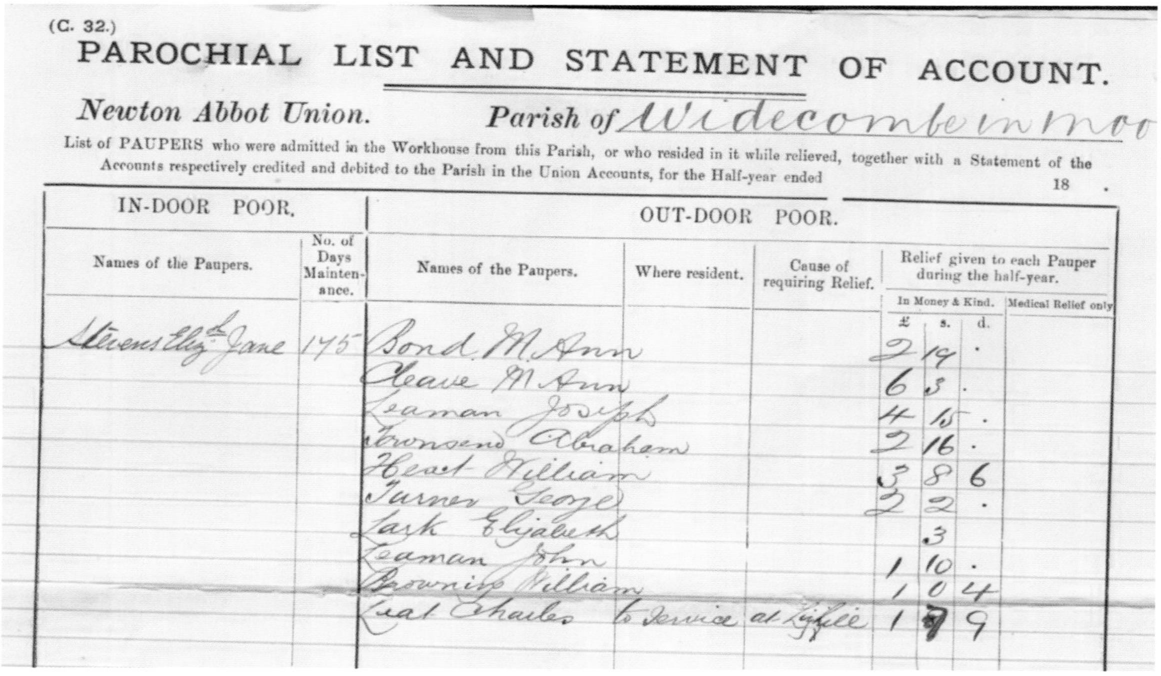
(C. 32.)

PAROCHIAL LIST AND STATEMENT OF ACCOUNT.

Newton Abbot Union. *Parish of* Widecombe in Moo

List of PAUPERS who were admitted in the Workhouse from this Parish, or who resided in it while relieved, together with a Statement of the Accounts respectively credited and debited to the Parish in the Union Accounts, for the Half-year ended 18 .

IN-DOOR POOR.		OUT-DOOR POOR.						
Names of the Paupers.	No. of Days Maintenance.	Names of the Paupers.	Where resident.	Cause of requiring Relief.	Relief given to each Pauper during the half-year. In Money & Kind. £	s.	d.	Medical Relief only
Stevens Eliz^th Jane	175	Bond M Ann			2	19	.	
		Cleave M Ann			6	3	.	
		Leaman Joseph			4	15	.	
		Townsend Abraham			2	16	.	
		Hext William			3	8	6	
		Turner George			2	2	.	
		Lark Elizabeth				3		
		Leaman John			1	10	.	
		Browning William			1	0	4	
		Leat Charles	to service	at Lyhill	1	7	9	

FIGURE 10-9: DETAIL FROM THE HALF-YEAR ENDING LADY DAY 1895 STATEMENT OF ACCOUNT OF NEWTON ABBOT UNION FOR THE PARISH OF WIDECOMBE

(IMAGE A046.025.P001 FROM THE WIDECOMBE ARCHIVE)

A partial transcript of Figure 10-9 is given below.

IN-DOOR POOR.

Names of the Paupers.	*No. of Days Maintenance.*
Stevens Eliz^th Jane	*175*

OUT-DOOR POOR.

Names of the Paupers.	*Where resident.*	*Cause of requiring Relief.*	*In Money & Kind.*	*Medical Relief only.*
Bond M Ann			*£2 19s 0d*	
Cleave M Ann			*£6 3s 0d*	
Leman Joseph			*£4 15s 0d*	
Townsend Abraham			*£2 16s 0d*	
Hext William			*£3 8s 6d*	
Turner George			*£2 2s 0d*	
Lark Elizabeth			*£0 3s 0d*	
Leman John			*£1 10s 0d*	
Browning William			*£1 0s 4d*	
Leat, Charles	*To service*	*At Lyhill*	*£1 7s 9d*	

Now there is only Elizabeth Jane Stevens residing in the workhouse at Newton. She, presumably, is a long-term resident. Unfortunately, once again the residency of the out-door poor is not specified.

Looking at the balance sheet for Michaelmas half-year 1895 (see Figure 10-10 and Figure 10-11), we note two things. Firstly, that there were two rates collected in that half-year, one in April and then again in July. Secondly, that there were various other expenses that could potentially be taken out of the poor rate, notably payments to the Sanitary Authority, the Highway Board, the School Board and the Burial Board. In other words, the Poor Rate is becoming much more of a general rate (it will be remembered that the collection of the County Rate has been a part of the Poor Rate from an early date).

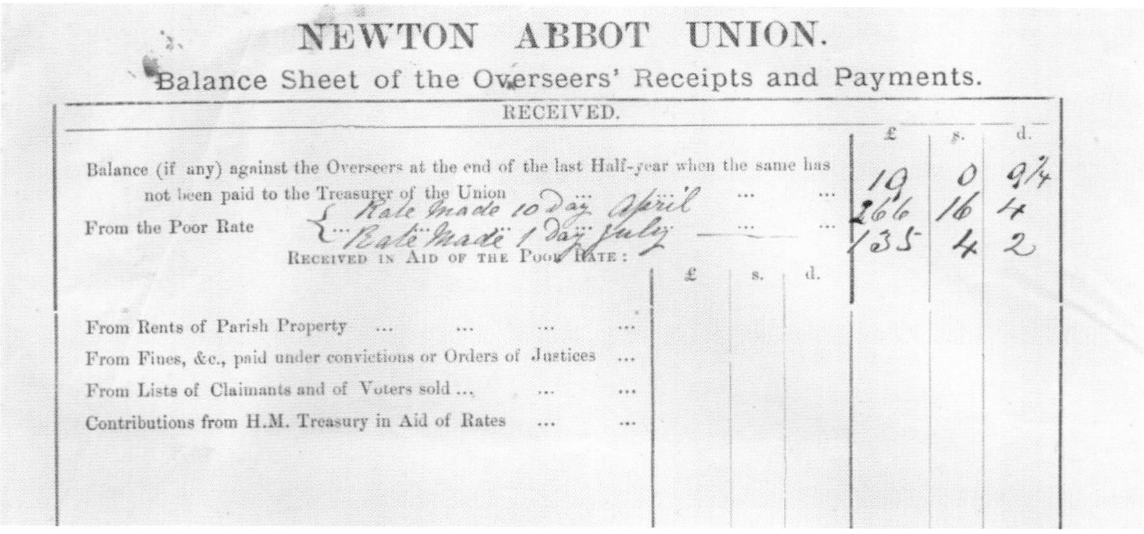

NEWTON ABBOT UNION.

Balance Sheet of the Overseers' Receipts and Payments.

RECEIVED.

	£	s.	d.
Balance (if any) against the Overseers at the end of the last Half-year when the same has not been paid to the Treasurer of the Union	10	0	9¼
From the Poor Rate { Rate made 10 day April	266	16	4
{ Rate Made 1 day July	135	4	2

RECEIVED IN AID OF THE POOR RATE:

	£	s.	d.
From Rents of Parish Property			
From Fines, &c., paid under convictions or Orders of Justices ...			
From Lists of Claimants and of Voters sold			
Contributions from H.M. Treasury in Aid of Rates			

FIGURE 10-10: DETAIL FROM THE HALF-YEAR BALANCE SHEET ENDING MICHAELMAS 1895 OF NEWTON ABBOT UNION FOR THE PARISH OF WIDECOMBE

(IMAGE A046.001.P001 FROM THE WIDECOMBE ARCHIVE)

It is worth noting at this point that 1894 was the year when a scandal engulfed the Newton Abbot Workhouse. There were reports of a straitjacket being in constant use, of inmates being tied to their beds resulting in at least one death, of fleas and

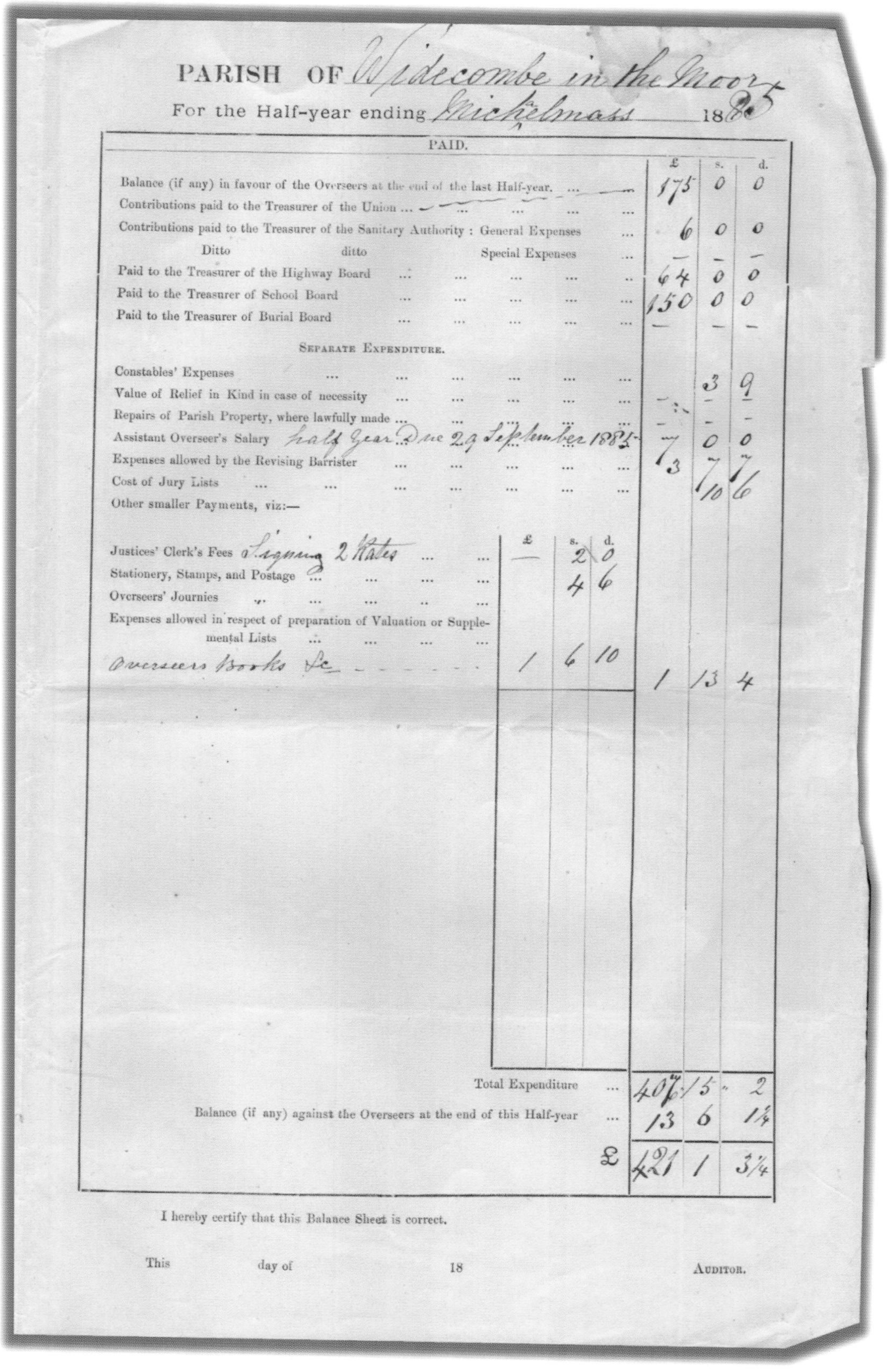

PARISH OF *Widecombe in the Moor*

For the Half-year ending *Michelmass* 18*95*

PAID.

	£	s.	d.
Balance (if any) in favour of the Overseers at the end of the last Half-year. ...	175	0	0
Contributions paid to the Treasurer of the Union			
Contributions paid to the Treasurer of the Sanitary Authority : General Expenses ...	6	0	0
Ditto ditto Special Expenses ...			
Paid to the Treasurer of the Highway Board	64	0	0
Paid to the Treasurer of School Board	150	0	0
Paid to the Treasurer of Burial Board			

SEPARATE EXPENDITURE.

	£	s.	d.
Constables' Expenses		3	9
Value of Relief in Kind in case of necessity			
Repairs of Parish Property, where lawfully made			
Assistant Overseer's Salary *half year Due 29 September 1885* ...	7	0	0
Expenses allowed by the Revising Barrister	3	7	7
Cost of Jury Lists		10	6
Other smaller Payments, viz:—			

	£	s.	d.			
Justices' Clerk's Fees *Signing 2 Rates*		2	0			
Stationery, Stamps, and Postage		4	6			
Overseers' Journies						
Expenses allowed in respect of preparation of Valuation or Supplemental Lists						
Overseers Books &c	1	6	10	1	13	4

	£	s.	d.
Total Expenditure ...	407	15	2
Balance (if any) against the Overseers at the end of this Half-year ...	13	6	1¼
£	421	1	3¼

I hereby certify that this Balance Sheet is correct.

This   day of   18   AUDITOR.

FIGURE 10-11: DETAIL FROM THE HALF-YEAR BALANCE SHEET ENDING MICHAELMAS 1895 OF NEWTON ABBOT UNION FOR THE PARISH OF WIDECOMBE

(IMAGE A046.001.P002 FROM THE WIDECOMBE ARCHIVE)

lice being commonplace, and various other horrific stories.[72] This became the subject of a local government enquiry and might be another explanation of why the numbers of inhabitants were down! Inmates and staff appear to be a lot happier by the time of Queen Victoria's Diamond Jubilee in 1897 (see Figure 10-2). Of course, appearances can be deceptive, but we know early photographers needed subjects to keep still for a while to get a sharp image – no scratching allowed!

Despite these problems, the work of the Newton Abbot Union continued for some time well into the 1900s and there are the odd reminders of it in the Widecombe Archive. As late as 1921 we have a document (reference M064.003) recording the payment of a Poor Rate to the Union (see Figure 10-12).

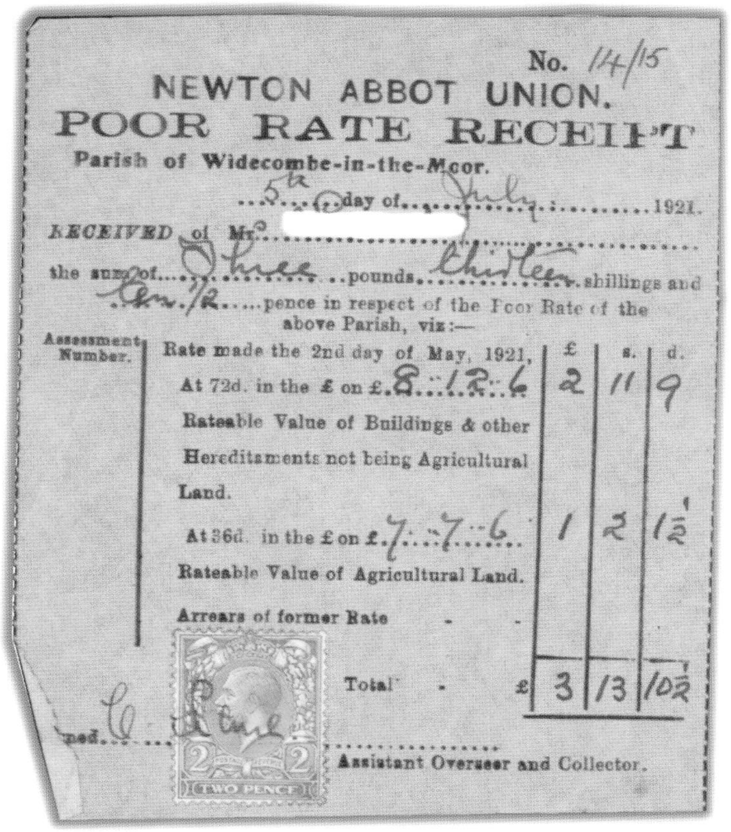

No. 14/15

NEWTON ABBOT UNION.

POOR RATE RECEIPT

Parish of Widecombe-in-the-Moor.

5th day of July 1921.

RECEIVED of Mr.

the sum of Three pounds thirteen shillings and Ten ½ pence in respect of the Poor Rate of the above Parish, viz:—

Assessment Number.		£	s.	d.
	Rate made the 2nd day of May, 1921, At 72d. in the £ on £ 8 : 12 : 6 Rateable Value of Buildings & other Hereditaments not being Agricultural Land.	2	11	9
	At 36d. in the £ on £ 7 : 7 : 6 Rateable Value of Agricultural Land.	1	2	1½
	Arrears of former Rate - -			
	Total - £	3	13	10½

Signed .... Assistant Overseer and Collector.

FIGURE 10-12: NEWTON ABBOT UNION POOR RATE RECEIPT FOR 5TH JULY 1921

(IMAGE M064.003 FROM THE WIDECOMBE ARCHIVE USED WITH PERMISSION - IMAGE IN PRIVATE OWNERSHIP)

There was also a payment of 'special expenses' at the same time (reference M064.004) (see Figure 10-13).

[72] Please see Price 2016, page 135-136 for more information and various other internet sites carry the story - search for 'Newton Abbot Union scandal'.

No. 14.15.

NEWTON ABBOT UNION.
SPECIAL EXPENSES RECEIPT.

Parish of Widecombe-in-the-Moor.

....5th....day of.......July..........1921.

RECEIVED of Mr..

the sum of.......—.......pounds.......four.......shillings and ......four......pence in respect of the Special Expenses Rate of the above Parish, viz:—

Assessment Number.		£	s.	d.
	Rate made the 2nd day of May, 1921, At 5d. in the £ on £.8.12.6. Rateable Value of Buildings & other Hereditaments not being Agricultural Land.		3	7
	At 5d. in the £ on £ 1.16.10½ Rateable Value of Agricultural Land.	-	-	9
	Arrears of former Rate - -			
	Total - £		4	4

Signed....C. Lane.............................
Assistant Overseer and Collector.

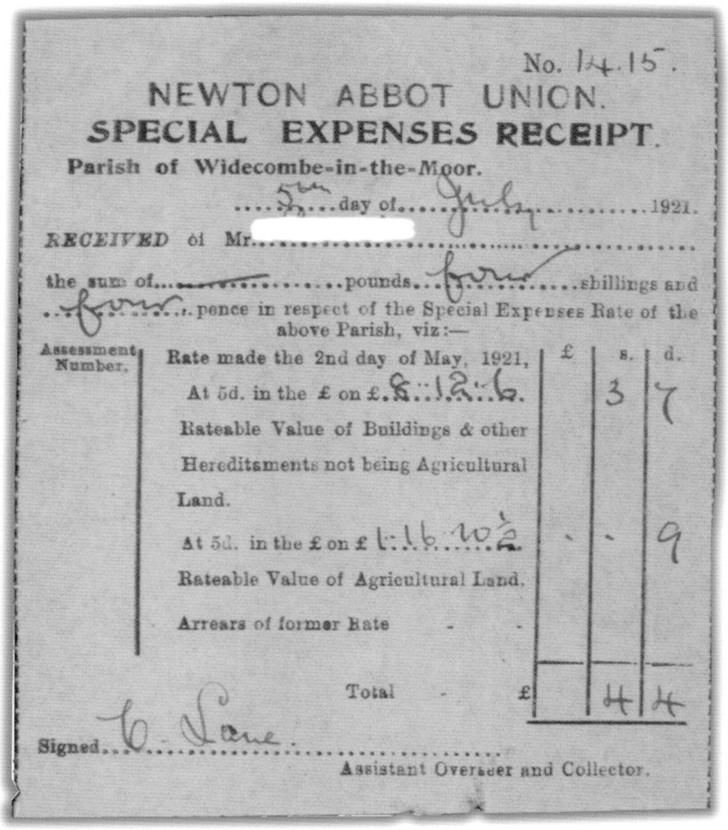

FIGURE 10-13: NEWTON ABBOT UNION SPECIAL EXPENSES RECEIPT FOR 5TH JULY 1921

(IMAGE M064.004 FROM THE WIDECOMBE ARCHIVE USED WITH PERMISSION - IMAGE IN PRIVATE OWNERSHIP)

In the burial register for Leusdon Church on 14th February 1884, Hannah Cribbett was buried at the age of 91 years and her address was given as Union House Newton Abbot (See Figure 10-14). So, even after death, the fact that someone from Widecombe is in the Newton Abbot Union Workhouse does not mean they are forgotten.

Hannah Cribbett. No. 67	Newton abbot Union House.	Feb. 14	91	John Williams Vicar of Widecombe

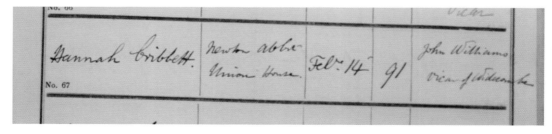

FIGURE 10-14: BURIAL OF HANNAH CRIBBETT ON 14TH FEBRUARY 1884, AGED 91, RECORDED IN LEUSDON CHURCH BURIAL REGISTER

(IMAGE C005.P009 FROM THE WIDECOMBE ARCHIVE USED WITH PERMISSION)

Given the events recorded above that occurred ten years after Hannah's burial, and that must have been going on for some time before they were discovered or acted upon, one wonders what sort of life Hannah had in the workhouse.

CHAPTER 11 OTHER WELFARE PROVISION

INTRODUCTION

The foregoing chapters cover the primary welfare provision for the parish. There are, however, some other areas that are worth touching on, partly out of interest, and partly because they indicate that provision was not necessarily limited to what was legally required and parishioners could also show initiative in making other provision for themselves and for the poor of the parish. Hence we see the setting up of charity schools for the poor of the parish and a number of friendly societies being formed to provide a measure of sickness benefit.

Finally, a brief mention is made of a further rate that was raised, the rate for the maintenance of the local highways. Getting about must always have been difficult on the moor, with packhorses and sledges being used rather than wheeled transport for transporting goods until much later than elsewhere, and horseback being the preferred mode of people transport,[73] and so maintenance of the King's Highways, apart from being a legal requirement, was clearly particularly important.

EDUCATION

The subject of education in Widecombe has been well covered elsewhere[74] and so will only be covered briefly here.

There were no doubt local, private or 'Dame' schools in the Widecombe parish but a major event occurred in 1796 or thereabouts when the Widecombe & Dartmoor Schools Charity was formed with the purpose of providing education for the poor children of the parish, including the Forest Quarter (see Stanbrook, 1991 page 68). The original Account Book for this charity was in the Widecombe Parish Chest and is now preserved at the SW Heritage Trust Devon Archives (Dartmoor and Widecombe Charity Schools, 1796-1875 - reference number 2955A/PF/1). This account book includes the rules of the charity which include: "That no child be admitted to this Charity whose parents can afford to pay for their instruction", which suggests that the poor of the parish are specifically targeted. The minimum

---

[73] And no doubt ultimately responsible for the demise of the Old Grey Mare in the song of Widecombe Fair.

[74] See Stanbrook 1991 and Ann Claxton's report

age is four and each child is entitled to three years instruction. After leaving school they were required to attend Sunday School, if living within a convenient distance.

FIGURE 11-1: 1814 INDENTURE RECORDING THE REVISED WIDECOMBE EDUCATION CHARITY
(IMAGE M012.001.F FROM THE WIDECOMBE ARCHIVE, IN PRIVATE OWNERSHIP, USED WITH PERMISSION)

The length of time to which each child was entitled to education coincided very nicely with the apprenticeship system, in that if a child was apprenticed out this would not be until the age of eight and from 1816 they had to be at least nine.

The opening pages of the Education Charity Account Book shows that schools were operating in:

- Venton with 10 scholars
- Ponsworthy with 10 scholars
- Merripit with 13 scholars
- Hexworthy with 7 scholars
- Hannaford with 6 scholars
- Withycombe Town with 2 scholars

The school at Withycombe Town may have been operating from the Church House. As we have noted elsewhere parts of the Church House were rented out for use as a school.

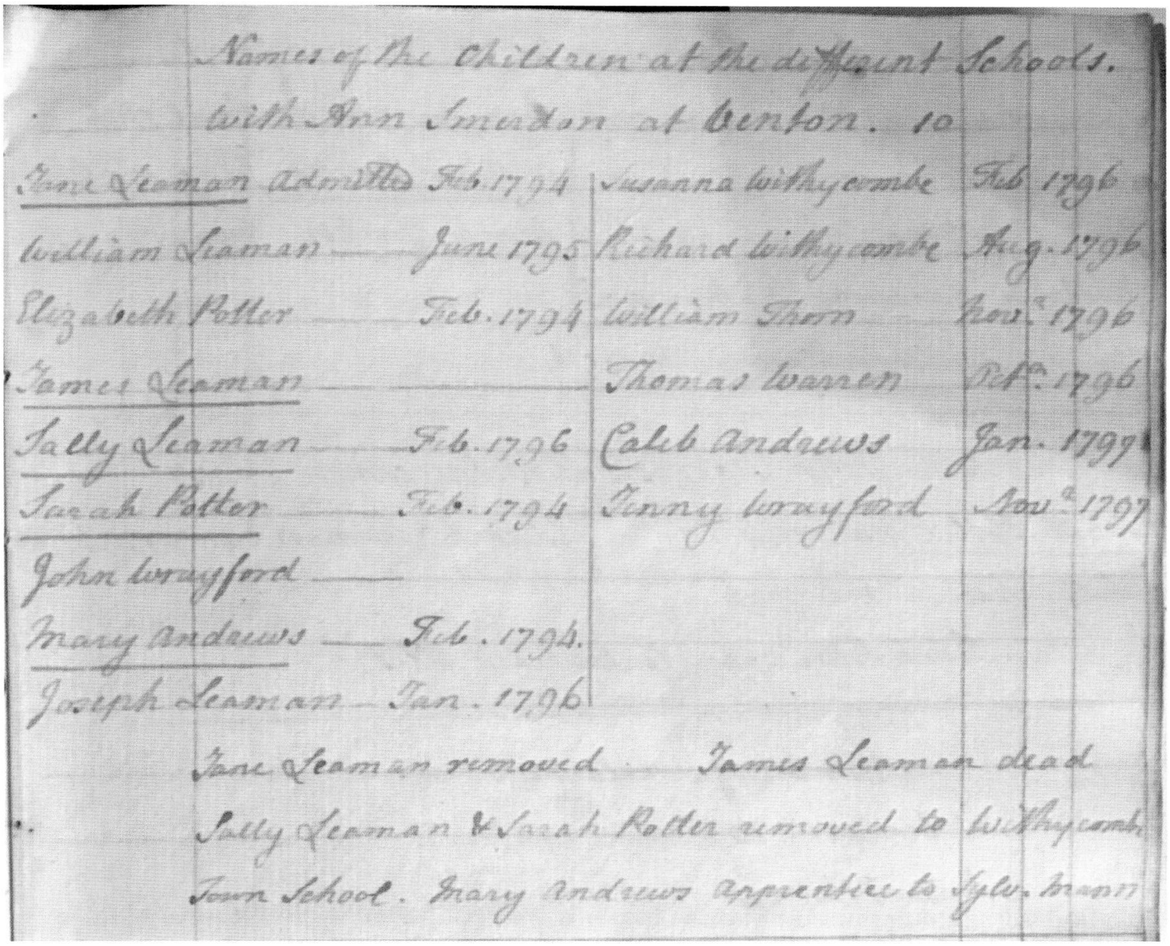
Names of the Children at the different Schools.
with Ann Smerdon at Venton. 10

Jane Leaman admitted	Feb. 1794	Susanna Withycombe	Feb 1796
William Leaman	June 1795	Richard Withycombe	Aug. 1796
Elizabeth Potter	Feb. 1794	William Thorn	Novr 1796
James Leaman		Thomas Warren	Octr 1796
Sally Leaman	Feb. 1796	Caleb Andrews	Jan. 1797
Sarah Potter	Feb. 1794	Jenny Wrayford	Novr 1797
John Wrayford			
Mary Andrews	Feb. 1794.		
Joseph Leaman	Jan. 1796		

Jane Leaman removed James Leaman dead
Sally Leaman & Sarah Potter removed to Withycombe Town School. Mary Andrews apprentice to Sylv. Mann

FIGURE 11-2: DETAIL FROM THE WIDECOMBE EDUCATION CHARITY ACCOUNT BOOK SHOWING THE NAMES OF THE CHILDREN IN THE SCHOOL AT VENTON 1796

(CATALOGUE ITEM (2955A/PF/1 FROM THE SW HERITAGE TRUST DEVON ARCHIVES)

Figure 11-2 shows the children in the school at Venton where the teacher was Ann Smerdon. Note the entry 'James Leaman dead'. There are one or two entries like this. Very sad to see. James must have died during the school year. There are also entries noting that a child has been apprenticed (or bound out) and therefore is no longer attending school - this is one reason for the annotation 'removed'. Children were also removed from one school to another. There is no indication or suggestion that this is any form of forced removal from school. Also note from this extract that some of the children were admitted in 1794, suggesting an earlier start for the charity than 1796 (or at least that some schools were already in existence in 1796).

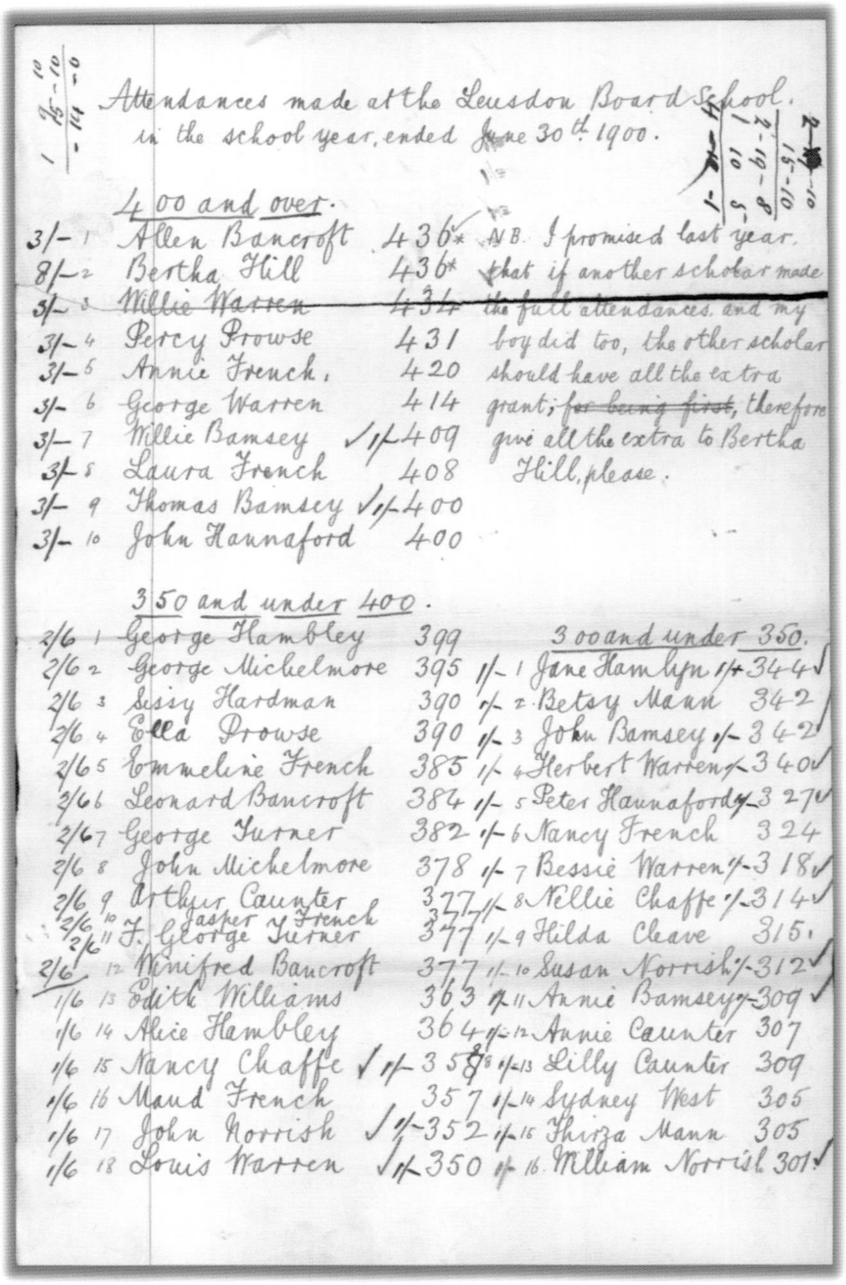

Attendances made at the Leusdon Board School.
in the school year, ended June 30th 1900.

400 and over.

3/- 1 Allen Bancroft 436* N.B. I promised last year
8/- 2 Bertha Hill 436* that if another scholar made
3/- 3 ~~Willie Warren 434~~ the full attendances and my
3/- 4 Percy Prowse 431 boy did too, the other scholar
3/- 5 Annie French 420 should have all the extra
3/- 6 George Warren 414 grant; ~~for being first~~, therefore
3/- 7 Willie Bamsey √1/- 409 give all the extra to Bertha
3/- 8 Laura French 408 Hill, please.
3/- 9 Thomas Bamsey √1/- 400
3/- 10 John Hannaford 400

350 and under 400. | 300 and under 350.

2/6 1 George Hambley 399
2/6 2 George Michelmore 395 1/- 1 Jane Hamlyn 1/- 344√
2/6 3 Sisiy Hardman 390 1/- 2 Betsy Mann 342
2/6 4 Ella Prowse 390 1/- 3 John Bamsey 1/- 342
2/6 5 Emmeline French 385 1/- 4 Herbert Warren 1/- 340√
2/6 6 Leonard Bancroft 384 1/- 5 Peter Hannaford 1/- 327√
2/6 7 George Turner 382 1/- 6 Nancy French 324
2/6 8 John Michelmore 378 1/- 7 Bessie Warren 1/- 318√
2/6 9 Arthur Caunter 377 1/- 8 Nellie Chaffe 1/- 314√
2/6 10 Jasper French 377 1/- 9 Hilda Cleave 315
2/6 11 F. George Turner
2/6 12 Winifred Bancroft 377 1/- 10 Susan Norrish 1/- 312√
1/6 13 Edith Williams 363 1/- 11 Annie Bamsey 1/- 309√
1/6 14 Alice Hambley 364 1/- 12 Annie Caunter 307
1/6 15 Nancy Chaffe √1/- 358 1/- 13 Lilly Caunter 309
1/6 16 Maud French 357 1/- 14 Sydney West 305
1/6 17 John Norrish √1/- 352 1/- 15 Thirza Mann 305
1/6 18 Louis Warren √1/- 350 1/- 16 William Norrish 301√

FIGURE 11-3 1900 ACCOUNT OF CALCULATION OF ATTENDANCE AT LEUSDON SCHOOL

There is also a later indenture recording the setting up of support for a charity school or schools in Widecombe (also including children from the Forest Quarter) - see Figure 11-1. This provides for an age range of boys and girls of not less than five and not more than eleven, and in reading until they reach the age of twelve. This probably represents an update to the original indenture as the allowed ages of the children are different.[75]

The children of parents who could afford to pay were not excluded from these schools, although attendance was presumably not compulsory. Instead they had to pay for their children to attend. So, the schools themselves probably took in a combination of charity and paid pupils. This may be why the charity is set up to pay the teacher for the children's attendance rather than to set up and run the schools themselves. This sounds a very sensible basis on which to operate as long as there was not a two-tier system in operation for the pupils. This would also explain why the Churchwardens could charge rent for the use of the Church House as a school: the teacher could pay this rent out of the fees that were charged to both parents and the charity. The charity enabled poor children to get some education which would otherwise be denied to them unless they were lucky.

An interesting aside to the payment to teachers is provided by the perhaps unique case of Leusdon School which was blessed with an endowment from Charlotte Larpent, who built the school and a teacher's residence. In Leusdon's case we have records showing that children were actually paid to attend school, presumably to discourage them (and their parents) from finding other ways to employ their time.

Figure 11-3 shows the calculation of attendance money. The target to reach for full attendance was 436 sessions that year and any child who reached that level received an extra 5 shillings, with those 400 and over receiving 3 shillings and so on down to 300 attendances. Allen Bancroft had received the bonus in the previous year, but this was probably unpopular and a tad unfair as he was, after all, the teacher's son!! The note on the right-hand-side of the image reads as follows:

"N.B. I promised last year that if another scholar made the full attendance and my boy did too, the other scholar should have all the extra grant, therefore give all the extra to Bertha Hill please."

So, in 1900 Bertha Hill receives the bonus and Willie Warren just missed out on a share by two days.

---

[75] M012 in the Widecombe Archive

SICKNESS BENEFIT

The problem of providing those in work with some form of protection from illness or accident before the days of employee or state benefits to help with those eventualities must have been a worrying one for every working person. Employment was much more insecure than today with most of it no doubt casual labour as and when required, so there was no sickness benefit and no, or very little, opportunity to save for the lean times - indeed probably _all_ the times were lean times.

The Rugglestone Friendly Society sprung from those concerns. It is interesting that this society was formed in 1836, the same time that the new Poor Law Acts came in. So you can imagine everyone feeling that these new poor laws, especially the parts that removed the responsibility for dispensing relief from local hands, necessitated some action by the local working population.

It was a form of insurance policy for those in work to provide something for them and their families if they became ill or otherwise unable to work. It was not a replacement for the poor relief, nor was it contributing to it, rather perhaps the working population felt that their chances of getting relief had been significantly reduced should they become incapacitated and so some form of local provision was called for.

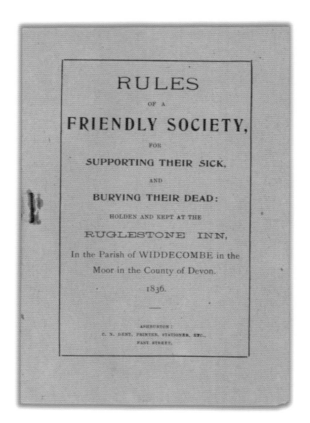

FIGURE 11-4: FRONT COVER OF THE RULES OF THE RUGGLESTONE FRIENDLY SOCIETY 1836

(IMAGE A015.002.P001 FROM THE WIDECOMBE ARCHIVE)

The cover page of the rules for the Rugglestone Friendly Society is shown in Figure 11-4

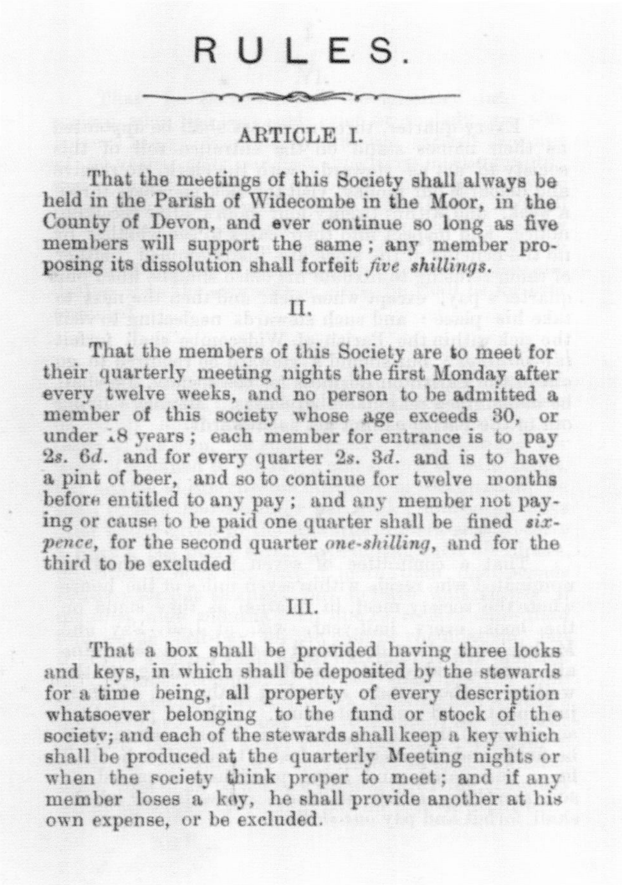

RULES.

ARTICLE I.

That the meetings of this Society shall always be held in the Parish of Widecombe in the Moor, in the County of Devon, and ever continue so long as five members will support the same; any member proposing its dissolution shall forfeit *five shillings.*

II.

That the members of this Society are to meet for their quarterly meeting nights the first Monday after every twelve weeks, and no person to be admitted a member of this society whose age exceeds 30, or under 18 years; each member for entrance is to pay 2*s.* 6*d.* and for every quarter 2*s.* 3*d.* and is to have a pint of beer, and so to continue for twelve months before entitled to any pay; and any member not paying or cause to be paid one quarter shall be fined *sixpence,* for the second quarter *one-shilling,* and for the third to be excluded

III.

That a box shall be provided having three locks and keys, in which shall be deposited by the stewards for a time being, all property of every description whatsoever belonging to the fund or stock of the society; and each of the stewards shall keep a key which shall be produced at the quarterly Meeting nights or when the society think proper to meet; and if any member loses a key, he shall provide another at his own expense, or be excluded.

FIGURE 11-5: FIRST PAGE OF THE RULES OF THE RUGGLESTONE FRIENDLY SOCIETY 1836

(IMAGE A015.002.P002 FROM THE WIDECOMBE ARCHIVE)

Rule II from Figure 11-5 states that new members must be between 18 and 30 years old and must be members for twelve months before becoming eligible to receive any benefit, apart from a pint of beer that they get at every meeting they attend once they have paid their dues!

At this point, it is perhaps worth mentioning Vancouver's observation that:

"However desirable it surely is to promote the extension of these societies, some regulation should still be made to restrain the men when assembled, from an indulgence which often ends in drunkenness. Would it not, therefore, be advisable to extend the forfeit to any one getting drunk during, or within 24 hours after, such monthly meetings?"[76]

Rule XXVII from Figure 11-6 makes the point that *"no pauper have any benefit from this Society,"* but a member who falls on bad times may be made *"a present".*

---

[76] Vancouver, 1808 Page 464

Catalogue item A015.002 in the Widecombe Archive has all the rules if the reader is interested in investigating further.

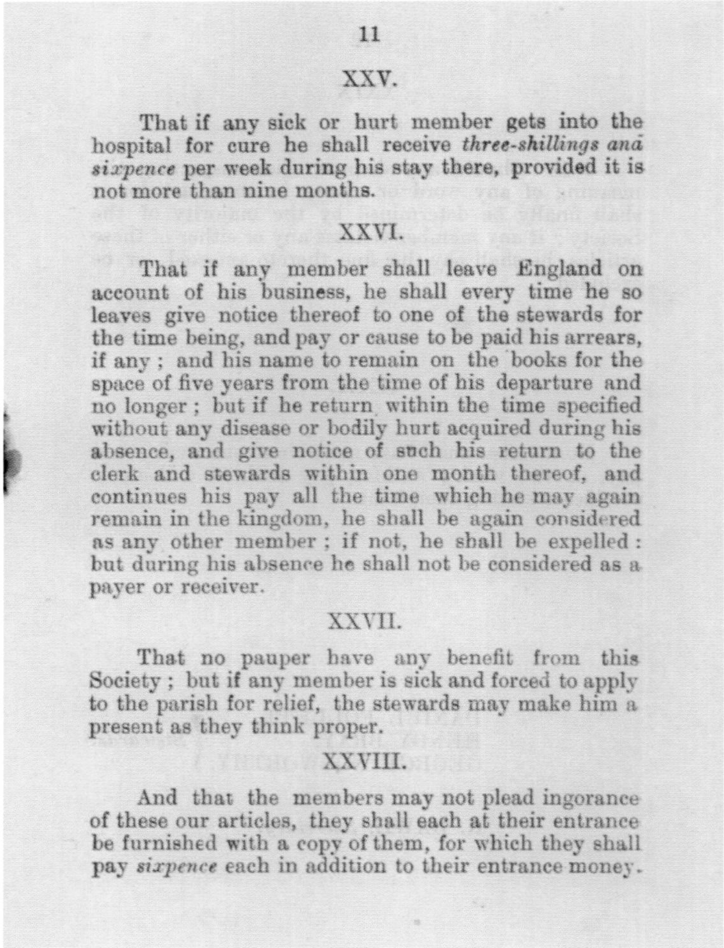

11

XXV.

That if any sick or hurt member gets into the hospital for cure he shall receive *three-shillings and sixpence* per week during his stay there, provided it is not more than nine months.

XXVI.

That if any member shall leave England on account of his business, he shall every time he so leaves give notice thereof to one of the stewards for the time being, and pay or cause to be paid his arrears, if any ; and his name to remain on the books for the space of five years from the time of his departure and no longer ; but if he return within the time specified without any disease or bodily hurt acquired during his absence, and give notice of such his return to the clerk and stewards within one month thereof, and continues his pay all the time which he may again remain in the kingdom, he shall be again considered as any other member ; if not, he shall be expelled : but during his absence he shall not be considered as a payer or receiver.

XXVII.

That no pauper have any benefit from this Society ; but if any member is sick and forced to apply to the parish for relief, the stewards may make him a present as they think proper.

XXVIII.

And that the members may not plead ingorance of these our articles, they shall each at their entrance be furnished with a copy of them, for which they shall pay *sixpence* each in addition to their entrance money.

FIGURE 11-6: PAGE 11 OF THE RULES OF THE RUGGLESTONE FRIENDLY SOCIETY 1836

(IMAGE A015.002.P006 FROM THE WIDECOMBE ARCHIVE)

FIGURE 11-7: DETAIL FROM JOHN WHITE'S RUGGLESTONE FRIENDLY SOCIETY RULEBOOK

(IMAGE A015.003.C FROM THE WIDECOMBE ARCHIVE)

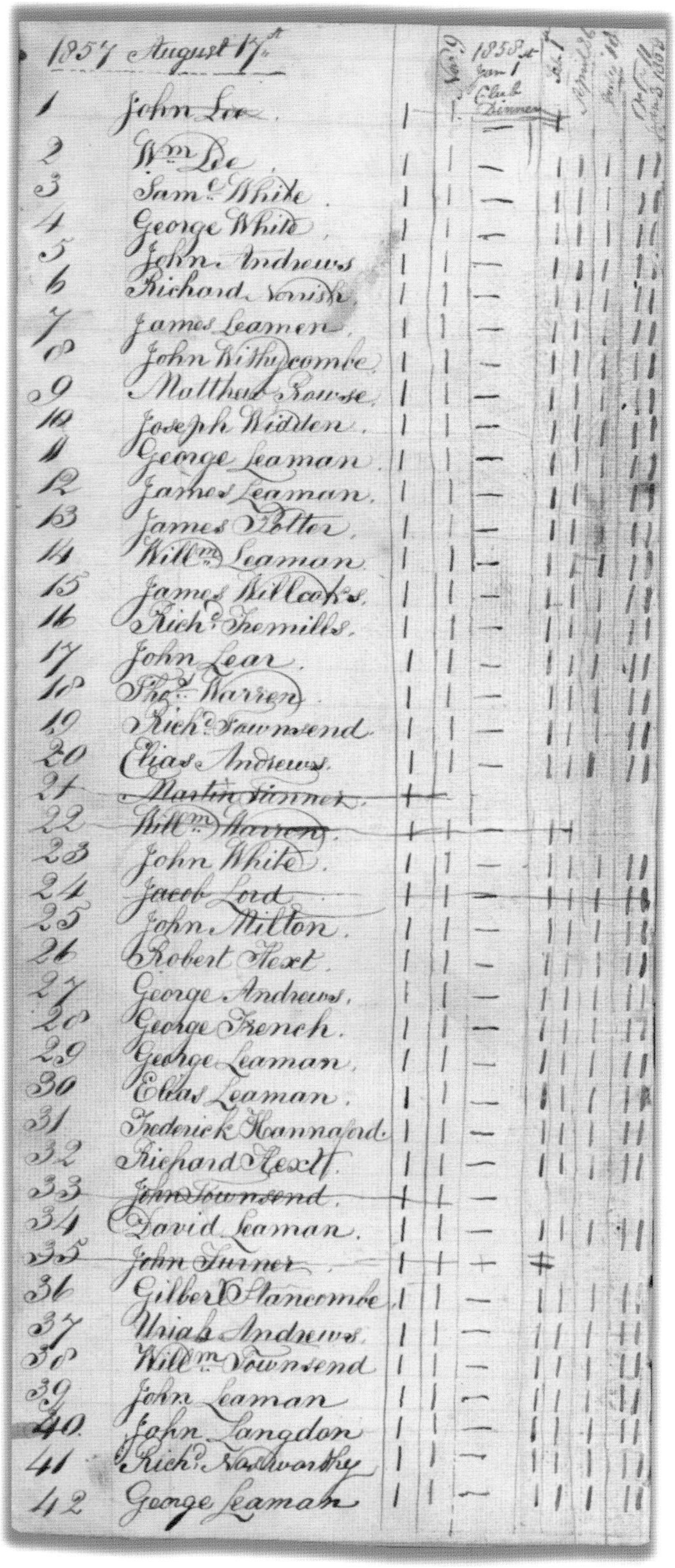
1857 August 17th

1 John Lee
2 Wm. Lee
3 Saml. White
4 George White
5 John Andrews
6 Richard Norrish
7 James Leamen
8 John Withycombe
9 Matthew Rowse
10 Joseph Widden
11 George Leaman
12 James Leaman
13 James Potter
14 Willm. Leaman
15 James Willcocks
16 Richd. Tremills
17 John Lear
18 Thos. Warren
19 Richd. Townsend
20 Elias Andrews
21 ~~Martin Turner~~
22 ~~Willm. Warren~~
23 John White
24 ~~Jacob Lord~~
25 John Milton
26 Robert Hext
27 George Andrews
28 George French
29 George Leaman
30 Elias Leaman
31 Frederick Hannaford
32 Richard Hext
33 ~~John Townsend~~
34 David Leaman
35 ~~John Turner~~
36 Gilbert Stancombe
37 Uriah Andrews
38 Willm. Townsend
39 John Leaman
40 John Langdon
41 Richd. Hamlyn
42 George Leaman

FIGURE 11-8: A PAGE SHOWING MEMBERS IN 1857 FROM THE MEMBERSHIP RECEIPT BOOK OF THE RUGGLESTONE FRIENDLY SOCIETY

(IMAGE A016.P001A FROM THE WIDECOMBE ARCHIVE)

Also in the Archive is John White's personal rulebook which has an interesting verse scribbled on the front page (see Figure 11-7) that reads as follows:

"Heaven is a happy place
    where God in glory dwell
I believe I shall be there
    and walk with him in white"

Amazingly, the records of the Rugglestone Friendly Society continue until 1992, when it was finally dissolved. The longevity of this Society is testament to the faithful nature of the people of Widecombe.

There was at least one other such society in the parish. One that crops up in one or two places in the archive, although there is little further detail, is the Poundsgate Amicable Society, which may have operated in a very similar way to the Rugglestone Friendly Society and been connected to it.

POOR RELIEF AS SICKNESS BENEFIT

Of course, a part of the dispensation of poor relief was to those who were sick or infirm as shown by the select vestry minutes for 30th November 1821 (see Figure 11-9).

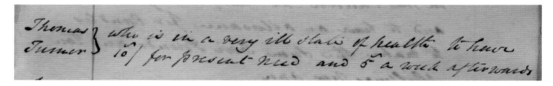

FIGURE 11-9: DETAIL FROM THE SELECT VESTRY MEETING OF 30TH NOVEMBER 1821 SHOWING THOMAS TURNER RECEIVING RELIEF BECAUSE OF THE STATE OF HIS HEALTH

(CATALOGUE ITEM 2955A/PV/1 PAGE 15 FROM THE SW HERITAGE TRUST DEVON ARCHIVES)

The transcript of Figure 11-9 is as follows:

"Thomas Turner
who is in a very ill state of health to have
10s/ for present need and 5s a week afterwards"

HIGHWAYS

It was mentioned in the Introduction that to include maintenance of the highways in 'welfare' might be stretching things a bit. However, communications were vitally important at a time when there was no telephone or public transport. What if there was a need to call a doctor? The probable method for doing this was to hire someone to make the trip for you (if you couldn't do it yourself) to call the doctor out. This is evidenced in the section on Medical Help in Chapter 7 where Dr Mogridge sends in his bill for numerous journeys to Widecombe from his home. Some of these journeys will have been planned, no doubt, but some might well have been as a result of a summons. The journey to Ashburton from Widecombe at that time, even on horseback, would have been time-consuming and decently maintained highways would have been very desirable.

So, it is interesting, that, as well as Tithes, the Poor Rate and the Church Rate there is a periodic rate raised for the maintenance of the Highways in the Parish and parishioners contribute to this rate in the same way that they contribute to the others. Once again, we see the forerunner of district, county and national rates and taxes operating at the local parish level.

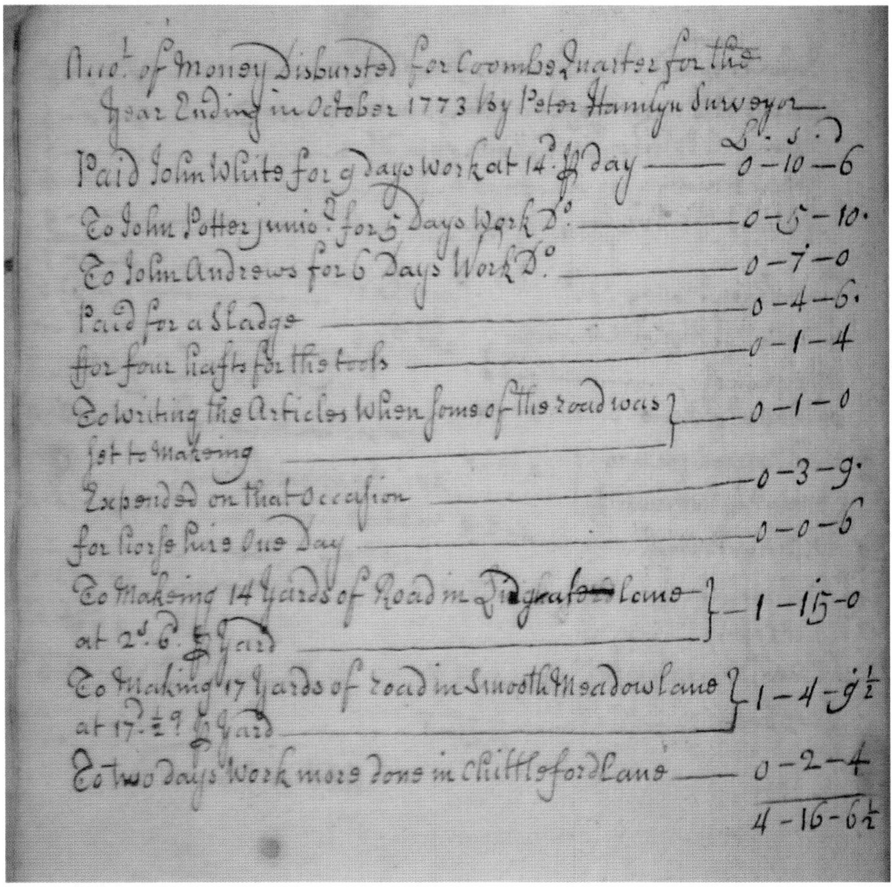

FIGURE 11-10: DETAIL FROM HIGHWAYS ACCOUNT BOOK FOR 1773 SHOWING SOME ACTIVITY FOR COOMBE (WIDECOMBE) QUARTER

(IMAGE A026.P021 FROM THE WIDECOMBE ARCHIVE)

An example of activity concerned with the repair of the highways is shown in Figure 11-10. It can be seen that most of the expenditure goes on labour and on making up sections of road. As mentioned above, it is worth remembering that much of the transportation of goods etc. at this time was probably carried out using a sledge pulled by a horse or by using pack-horses, i.e. wheeled transport would have been a rarity on the Moor.

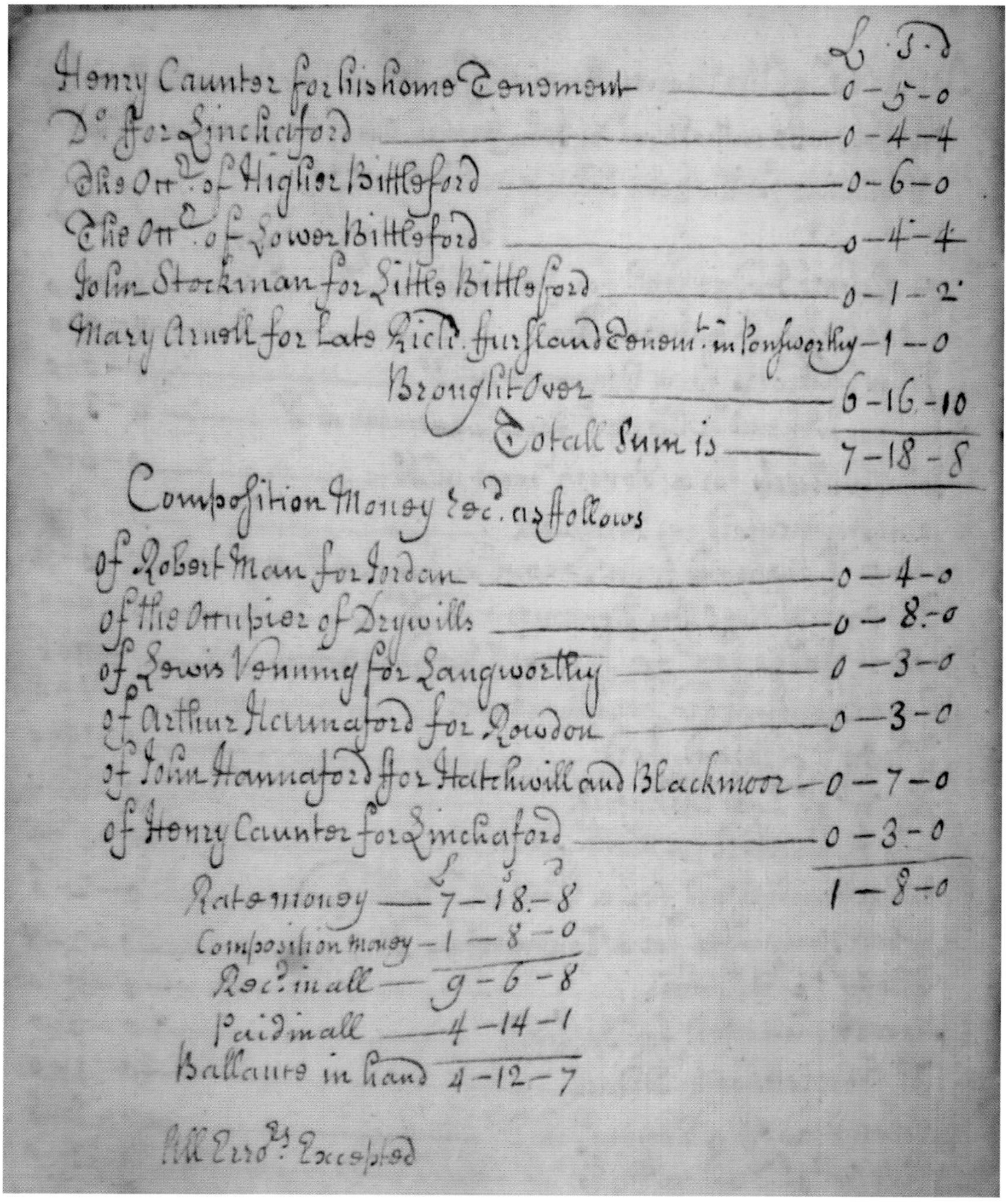

L s d
Henry Caunter for his home Tenement — 0-5-0
Do. for Lincicford — 0-4-4
The Occr. of Higher Bittleford — 0-6-0
The Occr. of Lower Bittleford — 0-4-4
John Stockman for Little Bittleford — 0-1-2
Mary Arnell for Late Richd. furzland Tenemt. in Ponsworthy — 1-0
Brought Over — 6-16-10
Totall Sum is — 7-18-8

Composition Money Recd. as follows
of Robert Man for Jordan — 0-4-0
of the Occupier of Drywills — 0-8-0
of Lewis Venning for Langworthy — 0-3-0
of Arthur Hannaford for Rowdon — 0-3-0
of John Hannaford for Hatchwill and Blackmoor — 0-7-0
of Henry Caunter for Lincicford — 0-3-0
1-8-0

L s d
Rate money — 7-18-8
Composition money — 1-8-0
Recd. in all — 9-6-8
Paid in all — 4-14-1
Ballance in hand 4-12-7

All Errors Excepted

FIGURE 11-11: DETAIL FROM HIGHWAYS ACCOUNT BOOK FOR 1773 SHOWING INCOME RECEIVED FROM PARISHIONERS

(IMAGE A026.P022 FROM THE WIDECOMBE ARCHIVE)

Figure 11-11 shows a detail of the money raised through the Highway Rate. There is also 'composition money' raised. It is hard to know what this is.

CHAPTER 12 THE NATIONAL CENSUS RETURNS

The first National census was carried out in 1841 and so we have no census information for the period prior to the formation of the Newton Abbot Union. However, some light might be shed on how the Church House was used in and after 1841 and where paupers were to be found, so some analysis of the returns is of value and as usual such study raises as many questions as are answered.

In 1841 no occupier is identified as a pauper, but then only limited information was collected in this first census. The Church House is not specifically named either. There is only the general description of 'Widecombe Village'. Only the occupation of the first named person for a property is given and that only when they have a recognised occupation. For instance, there is an Elizabeth Leaman, aged 60, recorded in one dwelling with the occupation of 'Errand Woman' and in 1851 Dinah Leaman aged 53 'Letter Receiver'. It is possible that a dwelling with a mixture of families and young and old alike might be being used as a poorhouse. For instance, there is a property with Mary and John Withycombe aged 5 and 3 respectively in a house with no other Withycombes and another with Mary Warren on her own with her four children. However, it is difficult to reach any firm conclusions.

The Church House is fairly well occupied until 1881, and, for example, even in 1861 it is divided into six households, although exactly what the division between them was other than the fact that they were different families is hard to determine. Some of those people are identified as paupers, although the building is not named as a poorhouse or workhouse. By 1881 there was one family left (that of Richard Nosworthy, Agricultural Labourer, presumably occupying the cottage at the west end), and one elderly lodger Mary Potter, who is possibly acting as some form of caretaker/housekeeper. The board school was established by this date in the Church House and that is listed as unoccupied.

None of the census returns up to 1901 lists the occupation of an inhabitant as 'Sexton'. Perhaps that was Richard Nosworthy's part-time occupation or perhaps it only became occupied by the Sexton later on.

There are numerous paupers listed as residing in houses in the parish. For instance, in Stout Cottage in 1861 there is Richard Leaman aged 59 and his family listed as a pauper, together with a lodger. There is also John Nosworthy aged 79 a pauper and his wife.

There are some particularly sad entries in the 1851 census. In Lower Town there is an entry for Abraham Stancomb aged 76, a pauper agricultural labourer and his wife Jenny aged 68. They are listed with Harriett their daughter aged 24 identified as a pauper cripple. Also in Lower Town in 1851 there is an entry for Samuel

Hannaford's grandson residing with the family aged 26 who is identified as a pauper (weak of mind).[77]

There are numerous other, mainly elderly, people listed as paupers. This prevalence of elderly paupers highlights an obvious fact that given that there was no automatic old age pension, the elderly were especially vulnerable to poverty, especially a wife whose working husband had died and so the Poor Law system was a valuable lifeline. This has the hallmarks of 'care in the community' where the elderly stay in their houses or perhaps with family, who on their own cannot afford to look after their relatives (perhaps they need medical care of one sort or another) and so the availability of some form of poor relief would be a godsend. Even though by this date the administration of the poor relief system had been taken over by the Newton Abbot Union there would still have been local involvement (as noted In Chapter 10 above). It also shows that prior to the Union (and the National censuses), this form of relief would have been common (so-called out-relief where those in need still lived out in the community).

As an indication of the extent to which children were being bound out as apprentices in Widecombe, a study of the 1841 census shows that there were at least thirty-four children recorded as apprentices across twenty farms and a further twenty-four children recorded as farm-labourers[78].

---

[77] According to the, later, 1881 census, Samuel had a sister, Joanna, also mentally impaired, who was resident in the Newton Abbot Union Workhouse.

[78] David Ashman (personal communication).

CHAPTER 13 THE RELATIONSHIP WITH LYDFORD

Lydford (or Lidford as it is usually spelt in documents in the Archive) is a Dartmoor parish that was located immediately to the west of Widecombe[79]. There was a long-standing agreement that people from Lydford who lived close to the Widecombe parish boundary and for whom the journey to Lydford Church was long and arduous, especially in winter, could use Widecombe Church instead of Lydford Church. This is the origin of local Widecombe features such as 'The Church Path' and the 'Coffin Stone'. The agreement dates back to Bishop Bronscombe's "Ordinacio de Lideford" dated 20th August 1260, which relates specifically to Babbeney[80] (Babeny) and Pushyll (Pizwell), a translation of which is quoted in Stephen Woods' book on page 35[81]. Another translation, dating from 1816, can be viewed at the Exeter Cathedral Archive[82]. The reasoning behind the agreement was that when someone died, for example, the task of carrying the coffin from close to the borders of Widecombe all the way across the moor to Lydford Church would have been extremely arduous, especially in winter, and so Widecombe Church was available for use instead. The coffin stone on Dartmeet Hill is so named because it was used to rest coffins (and their bearers!) on the way to Widecombe.

This agreement required those from those hamlets who used Widecombe Church to contribute to the upkeep etc. of Widecombe Church and they would therefore have been included in the raising of the various rates. Indeed, these areas are identified as the 'Forest Quarter' within the Churchwardens' and Overseers' Accounts and elsewhere. This Forest Quarter extended all the way to Two Bridges and included hamlets such as Pizwell, Hexworthy and Huccaby (in fact all the properties located in the East and South Quarters as shown in Figure 13-1). The Widecombe Overseers' Accounts record Poor Rates being collected from properties in this quarter right up until 1818 at which point the Forest Quarter ceases to be mentioned.

---

[79] This is no longer the case since the Dartmoor Forest Parish Council was formed in 1987, by the splitting of the parish of Lydford - see http://www.dartmoorforestpc.net/.

[80] Or 'Balbenye' in Stephen Woods' version.

[81] Woods, Stephen, 1996.

[82] Under Exeter Cathedral Archive reference D&C 4622/4.

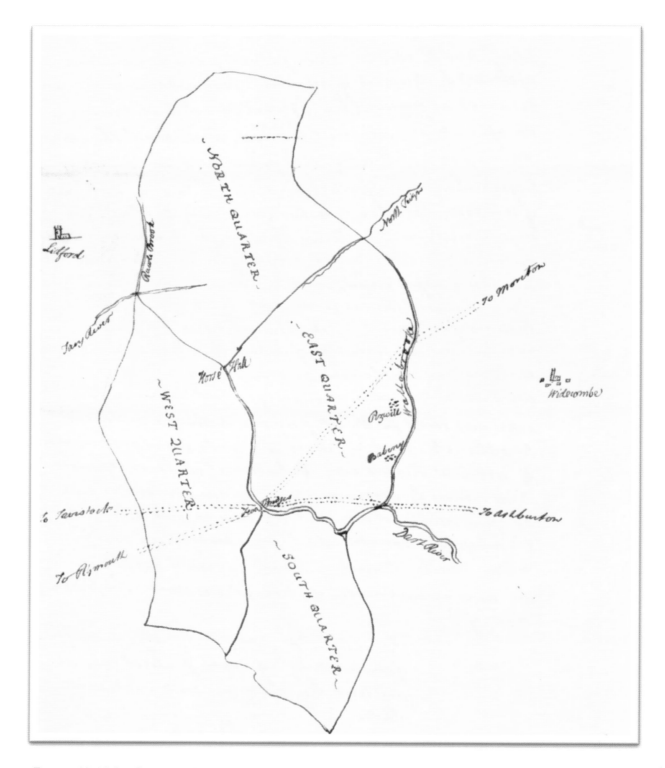

FIGURE 13-1 MAP SHOWING LYDFORD FOREST QUARTERS - FROM A DOCUMENT IN EXETER CATHEDRAL ARCHIVE DATED 6TH SEPTEMBER 1816

NOTE TWO BRIDGES AT THE CROSSROADS

(DOCUMENT REFERENCE D&C 4622/4 FROM THE EXETER CATHEDRAL ARCHIVE USED WITH PERMISSION)

The ceasing of the Poor Rate collection from the Forest Quarter suggests that the responsibility for the poor who were located there would have switched to Lydford by 1818. This is backed-up by a note at the foot of the map shown in Figure 13-1 which mentions the Poor Rate being transferred to Lydford, although it does not say why. This note is shown in Figure 13-2. Note that the Church Rate continues to be paid to Widecombe until about 1825, when it also disappears from the Widecombe records.

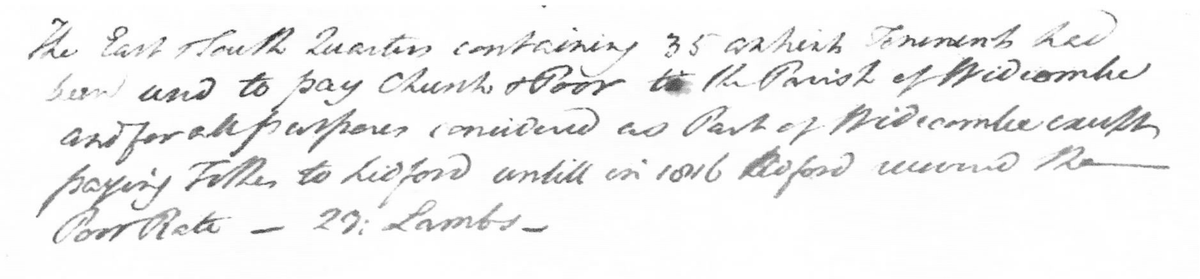

FIGURE 13-2 NOTE AT THE FOOT OF THE MAP IN FIGURE 13-1 - FROM A DOCUMENT IN EXETER CATHEDRAL ARCHIVE DATED 6TH SEPTEMBER 1816

(DOCUMENT REFERENCE D&C 4622/4 FROM THE EXETER CATHEDRAL ARCHIVE USED WITH PERMISSION)

The transcription of the note in Figure 13-2 is as follows:

The East & South Quarters containing 35 antient Tenements had
been used to pay Church & Poor to the Parish of Widcombe
and for all purposes considered as Part of Widecombe except
paying Tithes to Lidford untill in 1816 Lidford received the
Poor Rate - 27: Lambs.

The Exeter Cathedral Archive also has a record of a legal action brought in 1816, the purpose of which was to contest the boundaries of the parishes of Widecombe and Lydford[83]. This was brought by a Mr. Norris of Huccaby who argued that Poor Rates etc. had been paid to Widecombe for as long as he could remember and for many years before, and therefore, in fact, Huccaby lay within Widecombe Parish rather than within Lydford Parish. Various documents were produced, however, including the 1260 decree of the Bishop referred to above, that showed that the Forest Quarters were in fact part of Lydford Parish but that the inhabitants of these Quarters were allowed to use Widecombe Church as a convenience and no parish boundary change had occurred as a result. It is possible that this action was the trigger for the Poor Rate to revert to Lydford as the various events related here all occurred at approximately the same time. However, direct evidence of this has not so far been found.

Those poor who were within the Widecombe Poorhouse who were from the Forest Quarter (if any) could possibly have been transferred to Lydford at this time, although no direct evidence of this has been found either and it might in any case have been difficult to do and especially to identify who might fall into that category.

Also was someone living in the Forest Quarter legally settled in Lydford or Widecombe? Poor rates were paid to Widecombe from the Forest Quarter and poor

---

[83] Exeter Cathedral Archive Document D&C 4622/4: Report of the Action of Norris vs. Kelly and Saville dated to 1816

relief was dispensed from Widecombe to the Forest Quarter. Furthermore, someone living in the Forest Quarter could at some point have relocated to one of the Widecombe quarters and vice-versa. All in all, it could get very confusing.

These complications might also explain why, if a pauper could legitimately be removed to Lydford, then the Overseers would try hard to do so, even if it meant potential hardship for the person concerned - see George Leaman in Chapter 9 Removal Orders. George's parents were from Lydford although they had lived in Widecombe for a long time and indeed they were married during the period that the Forest Quarter was a part of Widecombe and so may have fallen into one of the categories discussed above. It should be noted, however, that their place of residence in Lydford Parish is not known.

CHAPTER 14 CONCLUSIONS

Although Widecombe has a very good collection of documents from the period being studied in this book, they are all factual records as required largely by law. There are no personal accounts that would have provided insights into how people felt or what they were thinking. It would have been amazing to come across a personal memoir such as 'My year as an Overseer', or 'What it is like to be on the receiving end of poor-relief' or something similar, but sadly this has not happened so far! Generally, in those days, and in a rural community in particular, such reflections did no doubt occur, but predominantly in conversation and in the mind, rather than on paper. The closest thing we have is the select vestry minutes which do record the odd emotional occurrence, such as the family that resisted their child being bound as an apprentice[84] and the woman who held out for a larger allowance.[85] But these minutes do not explain the reasons behind decisions. For instance, there are numerous notes in the minutes that pay is to be reduced for an individual but no explanation as to why.

Furthermore, the no doubt voluminous documents backing up the accounts appear without exception to have been lost. There was no reason to retain them once the accounts had been signed off and so they were not retained (this was common practice according to South West Heritage Trust). Nonetheless, the records that have survived provide a comprehensive picture of what poor and other relief was provided locally and although we do not get to hear about those who just miss out on this relief or those who perhaps fall foul of the Overseers or their agents, and no doubt there were numerous conflicts and disagreements, in general terms matters appear to have been fairly well organised and carefully implemented over a considerable period of time, which is testament to the diligence of the people of Widecombe parish given its relatively isolated moorland location.

There is a general feeling emanating from the text that, once the 1836 Poor Law revisions took hold, and the Newton Abbot Union took over, that the situation for those in receipt of poor relief deteriorated somewhat. Decisions were no longer locally made and so were made by strangers in many cases. Newton Abbot must have seemed a long way away to most Widecombe people and this must have acted as a deterrent, with any application for relief having become less local in nature, even with a locally appointed Guardian of the Poor. Overall, there appears to be a much less comfortable feeling, and perhaps this was the intention and part of the reasoning behind the changes. The de-personalising of welfare is of course

---

[84] See Figure 8-9 and Figure 8-10.

[85] See Figure 7-8.

something that continues to this day, with 'officialdom' and an anonymous bureaucracy very much in the forefront of the decision-making process.

In many ways the present volume has only scratched the surface. The author was conscious of the importance of keeping the book to a reasonable length and so a selective approach has been adopted. The use of web pages to supplement the material (e.g. to provide a full transcript of certain Overseers' Accounts)[86] has helped in this regard and as more work is carried out these web pages will expand to provide more background information.

It is also hoped that readers will be inspired to do their own investigations, perhaps following a particular person, or possible ancestor, to see what might have happened to them. There are so many stories in these records, despite their factual nature. These stories are all just waiting to be unearthed and told. Good luck!

---

[86] See Appendix A and Appendix B

APPENDICES

APPENDIX A THE TRANSCRIPT OF THE OVERSEERS' ACCOUNTS FOR 1804

This Appendix provides access to a full transcript of the Overseers' Accounts covering the calendar year 1804, as an example of the complexity of the task facing the Overseers, and out of interest for the wealth of information provided.

The Accounts run from approximately Easter to the following Easter. Therefore, in order to include the calendar year 1804, and for completeness, two sets of Overseers' Accounts are provided:

- 1803-1804
- 1804-1805

Due to the length of these accounts, the transcripts are located online. To access the transcripts, please use the following link:

https://www.widecombearchive.org.uk/welfare

This will take you to the full list of documents for which transcripts are available.

To view the Overseers' Accounts from this overall index, please click on 'Overseers Accounts'.

This takes you to the index page for the Overseers' Accounts. The years available are as mentioned above, that is, 1803-4 and 1804-5. To go directly to this index page you will need to use:

https://www.widecombearchive.org.uk/welfare/overseers_accounts

The Overseers' Accounts for 1803-1804, in common with all the other years, have a story on virtually every page. For instance, on page 7 (near the beginning of the financial year) there is a two-week payment made for Elizabeth Potter's second bastard child and the costs of a journey to the doctor for the child. In the same month they are burying the poor child and the accounts show the costs of a burying suit, of 'laying forth', making a grave, paying the minister plus some other expenses at the burial (perhaps refreshments?). On page 23 (towards the end of the account year) there is another reference to a coffin for Elizabeth Potter's child, but no other expenses are recorded this time.

There are various entries for the payment of bounty. This must relate to the Devon Militia that was manned by random selection and attendance was compulsory unless a fine was paid. Presumably this is what the 'bounty' is referring to. A substitute could also be provided, perhaps with a payment inducement. There is at least one example of this within the accounts.

APPENDIX B THE TRANSCRIPT OF THE CHURCHWARDENS' ACCOUNTS FOR 1804

This Appendix provides access to a full transcript of the Churchwardens' Accounts covering the calendar year 1804.

The Accounts run from approximately Easter to the following Easter. Therefore, in order to include the calendar year 1804, and for completeness, two sets of Churchwardens' Accounts are provided:

- 1803-1804 (known as the 1804 accounts)
- 1804-1805 (known as the 1805 accounts)

Due to the length of these accounts, the transcripts are located online. To access the transcripts, please use the following link:

https://www.widecombearchive.org.uk/welfare

This will take you to the full list of documents for which transcripts are available.

To view the Churchwardens' Accounts from this overall index, please click on 'Churchwardens Accounts'.

This takes you to the index page for the Churchwardens' Accounts. The years available are as mentioned above, that is, 1803-4 and 1804-5. To go directly to this index page you will need to use:

https://www.widecombearchive.org.uk/welfare/churchwardens_accounts

APPENDIX C THE EPISCOPAL VISITATION RETURN FOR WIDECOMBE IN THE MOOR, 1744

There follows the Text of the Episcopal Visitation Return for Widecombe in the Moor, 1744.

This text is taken from the Friends of Devon Archives website which provides a transcript of the full Returns for Devon.

http://www.foda.org.uk/visitations/1744/Chanter225B/Widecombe%20in%20the%20Moor.htm

Wythecombe in the Moor, Deanery of Moreton

Chanter 225B, 555-556

Population and dissenters: There are about an Hundred & five Families in my Parish. There is no Dissenter of any Denomination in my Parish.

Public or charity schools: There is not any publick or Charity School, endow'd or maintain'd in my Parish.

Alms-house, hospital or charitable endowment: There is an Alms-house in my Parish, but no Hospital or other Charitable endowment. There have not any Lands been left to ye Repair of ye Church or any other pious use, excepting one little Meadow about an Acre antiently given for ye Relief of ye poor, which ye Parishioners leas'd out for three Lives before I came to ye Parish.

Residence upon cure: I do reside personally upon my Cure, about half of a Mile from ye Church, but not at present in my Vicarage House which I have lately rebuilt.

Curate: [No answer given]

Divine service at other churches: No.

Frequency of divine service: On all publick Days, viz, ye 30th of January, 20th of May, Good-Friday &c. and twice every Lord's Day with a Sermon in ye Morning & Afternoon.

Frequency of communion: Five times.

Number of communicants: I have generally at Communion between three & four score sometimes more, at Easter last I had between fourscore & Ninety.

Catechising of children: I [illegible deletion] catechize ye Children in my Church, either ye 6th Sundays in Lent, or 6 Sundays after Whitsunday.

Chapels or chapels in ruins: There is not any Chapel within my Parish either standing, or in Ruins.

Thomas Granger

Widecombe V.... Thomas Granger, A.B.

inst. June 21. 1736. Presb. June 20 1736

Stephen Exon.

APPENDIX D USING THE WIDECOMBE DIGITAL ARCHIVE

The Widecombe Digital Archive is located at:

https://www.widecombearchive.org.uk

Go to the site and spend some time exploring the menu across the top which provides some background information on the project and on the various collections.

WHY COLLECTIONS?

Dividing the archive into collections is convenient as it allows for the breaking down into distinct parts of what otherwise would be a large monolithic archive. For example, the contents of the parish chest are quite separate from the History Group archive and therefore can be viewed in isolation. As there is a facility to combine all the collections together for searching, this segregation does not affect a user's ability to search the full archive.

You can get familiar with the various collections and their contents either from the Collections page:

https://www.widecombearchive.org.uk/collections.php

Or from the panel on the right-hand-side of most pages.

The Collections page is shown in Figure D-1.

FIGURE D-1: THE WIDECOMBE DIGITAL ARCHIVE COLLECTIONS PAGE

(COPYRIGHT WIDECOMBE HISTORY GROUP)

The collections available at the time of writing are as follows:

- Main Parish Archive (Parish Chest plus some baptisms and burials) -
  https://www.widecombearchive.org.uk/main_archive.php
- The Parish Apprenticeships -
  https://www.widecombearchive.org.uk/indentures.php
- The Tithe Apportionments -
  https://www.widecombearchive.org.uk/tithe_apportionments.php
- Widecombe Church Headstones -
  https://www.widecombearchive.org.uk/widecombe_headstones.php
- Widecombe History Group Archive -
  https://www.widecombearchive.org.uk/history_group_archive.php

WHAT INFORMATION IS AVAILABLE TO SEARCH?

The digitising project scanned paper-based images from documents in the physical archive and then catalogued those images. The cataloguing captured relevant information from the documents such as date, place and people together with other pieces of information that were considered of interest. Although the process was standardised, choosing items to catalogue is a somewhat subjective process and so uniform results are not always possible.

The catalogue generally retains the spelling used in the documents. Words (especially names and places) were often written as they sounded, so the documents contain a lot of variation in the spelling of local names and places. The search facility uses the concept of a 'synonym' to cater for these numerous spellings of a single name.

Importantly, many documents have not yet been catalogued in detail. For instance, the Churchwardens' and Overseers' Account Books were scanned and basic information used for cataloguing but no names were extracted at that time. There were many hundreds of pages of information and the task of going through each one to extract the names was too large a task, so the focus was on securing the information via a high-resolution image. The intention was that full extraction of names etc. could happen at a later date, perhaps when automated hand-writing recognition became available to speed up the process. And so, at present, searches in the Churchwardens' and Overseers' Accounts by name will not return any results.

Having said that, the accounts for 1804 and 1805 *have* been transcribed as an example of the content of this material. Details of those transcriptions are provided in Appendix A and Appendix B.

The decision was also taken to restrict the information available online of anything that was less than 100 years old. Anything of a personal, unpublished nature had to be at least 100 years old with newer items being restricted to public domain material such as photographs, programmes, posters etc. The full archive is kept under Widecombe History Group control.

How do I search?

Some examples are provided below to help the reader use the search facilities. Additional information is provided on the website under 'Help' in the main menu bar.

The best place to start a search is to choose 'Search the Collections' from the right-hand menu. This takes you to the main search page:

https://www.widecombearchive.org.uk/arch_display20.php

You can also get to this page from various other places on the site, or by clicking on the 'Details' link on any of the Collections pages alongside the list of individual items in the Collection.

FIGURE D-2: THE WIDECOMBE DIGITAL ARCHIVE SEARCH AND DISPLAY PAGE

(COPYRIGHT WIDECOMBE HISTORY GROUP)

Once on the Search page you need to choose the collection you wish to search in, or, if you are not sure which collection, click on the 'Combined' button on the right-hand-side. This joins all the collections together and searches them as one.

You can then choose either a basic search, a name search, or an advanced search.

BASIC SEARCH

This does what its name implies, i.e. you enter a value in the 'Search for' box and optionally another value in the 'and (optionally)' box and then click on the 'Search' button. Normally a value is a single word, with no spaces or other special characters, but multiple words separated by spaces will work as long as they match the corresponding string of characters in the collections.

The site will search the selected collection or collections for the values provided and will return a list of the items that contain the value or values that you have entered.

You can then browse the list that has been returned and select any for more detailed viewing by clicking on the 'More Details' button on the right-hand-side of the row that is of interest.

Basic Search: Show/Hide Tips

Search for: nosworthy   and (optionally): jane   Search   Clear Form

FIGURE D-3: THE WIDECOMBE DIGITAL ARCHIVE BASIC SEARCH BOX

(COPYRIGHT WIDECOMBE HISTORY GROUP)

For instance, I might be interested in seeing how many entries there are that contain the word 'nosworthy' (note that whether upper or lower case is immaterial), and the name 'jane', so I enter these in the first and second boxes, see Figure D-3. From the entries returned, at the time of writing, there were fifteen documents that matched (see Figure D-4).

Search Results:

You can look at details for an individual entry by clicking on the 'More Details' button next to the entry.

Total Number of Items Found: 15 Displaying Page 1 of 1   Go to Page: 1 ⬍ First Page Previous Page Next Page Last Page

Catalogue Number	Type of Item	Brief Description	Date(s) of Item	Images	More
A029.p153	Ledger	Surveyors of the Highways Account Book for the Parish of Widecombe - Division of Dudon (Jordan) - pages 11 to 15 of account year 1844-45	11.4.1844 - 10.4.1845	10	More Details
C001.002	Baptism Register	Register of Baptisms for the Parish of Widecombe in the Moor 1894-present day, page 2, 26.11.1895-13.12.1896	26.11.1895 - 13.12.1896	1	More Details
C001.012	Baptism Register	Register of Baptisms for the Parish of Widecombe in the Moor 1894-present day, page 12, 12.5.1907-27.11.1907	12.5.1907 - 27.11.1907	1	More Details
C001.013	Baptism Register	Register of Baptisms for the Parish of Widecombe in the Moor 1894-present day, page 13, 30.1.1908-27.9.1909	30.1.1908 - 27.9.1909	1	More Details
C004.041	Baptism Register	Register of Baptisms for St John the Baptist Church, Leusdon, 1863-present day, page 41, 16.12.1896 - 29.3.1898	14.12.1896 - 29.3.1898	1	More Details
C004.043	Baptism Register	Register of Baptisms for St John the Baptist Church, Leusdon, 1863-present day, page 43, 30.10.1898 - 26.11.1899	30.10.1898 - 26.11.1899	1	More Details
C004.044	Baptism Register	Register of Baptisms for St John the Baptist Church, Leusdon, 1863-present day, page 44, 7.1.1900 - 28.7.1901	7.1.1900 - 28.7.1901	1	More Details
A052.082	Indenture	Indenture of Elizabeth Brock dated 3.12.1822	3.12.1822	2	More Details
A052.295	Indenture	Indenture of Thomas Tremills dated 24.12.1802	24.12.1802	2	More Details
A052.298	Indenture	Indenture of Richard Leaman (b 1794) dated 22.10.1802	22.10.1802	2	More Details
P002.B28	Headstone	Headstone of Mary Jane Nosworthy. Date: 08.Feb.1905	08.02.1905	3	More Details
H346.001	Receipts & Lists	Accounts Papers concerning Leusdon & Widecombe School including attendances and payments to pupils, 1901	1901 - 1902	8	More Details
H346.002	Receipts & Lists	Accounts Papers concerning Leusdon & Widecombe School Fund including attendances and payments to pupils, 1902	1902	7	More Details
H346.003	Receipts & Lists	Accounts Papers concerning Leusdon & Widecombe School Fund including attendances and payments to pupils, 1903	1903	5	More Details
H346.004	Receipts & Lists	Accounts Papers concerning Leusdon & Widecombe School Fund including attendances and payments to pupils, 1904,1909,1910	1904 - 1910	8	More Details

Total Number of Items Found: 15 Displaying Page 1 of 1   Go to Page: 1 ⬍ First Page Previous Page Next Page Last Page

FIGURE D-4: THE WIDECOMBE DIGITAL ARCHIVE SEARCH AND DISPLAY PAGE - SEARCH RESULTS

(COPYRIGHT WIDECOMBE HISTORY GROUP)

If I choose A029.p153 (the Surveyors of the Highways Account Book for Dudon Quarter account year 1844-1845) for further examination, after clicking on 'More Details' I will see a document page as in Figure D-5.

FIGURE D-5: THE WIDECOMBE DIGITAL ARCHIVE DETAILED INFORMATION FOR A CATALOGUE NUMBER A029.P153

(COPYRIGHT WIDECOMBE HISTORY GROUP)

The information returned includes the names shown in Figure D-6. In this case the names occurring in the account book have been listed in the catalogue (unlike the Churchwardens' and Overseers' Accounts we discussed earlier).

Name: Lambles, Role: Roadman Address: Not Recorded Note: Not Recorded

Name: Hannaford, Roger Role: Roadman Address: Not Recorded Note: Not Recorded

Name: Warren, Joseph Role: Roadman Address: Not Recorded Note: Not Recorded

Name: Hannaford, Role: Surveyor Address: Not Recorded Note: Not Recorded

Name: Kitson, Thomas Role: Overseer Address: Not Recorded Note: Not Recorded

Name: Hale, W Role: Overseer Address: Not Recorded Note: Not Recorded

Name: Nosworthy, Jane Role: Overseer Address: Not Recorded Note: Not Recorded

Name: Lamble, Samuel Role: Overseer Address: Not Recorded Note: Not Recorded

Name: Hannaford, William Role: Overseer Address: Not Recorded Note: Not Recorded

Name: White, John Role: Overseer Address: Not Recorded Note: Not Recorded

Name: Smerdon, John Role: Overseer Address: Not Recorded Note: Not Recorded

FIGURE D-6: THE WIDECOMBE DIGITAL ARCHIVE DETAIL FROM THE 'DETAILED INFORMATION FOR CATALOGUE ENTRY A029.P153'

(COPYRIGHT WIDECOMBE HISTORY GROUP)

And it can be seen that Jane Nosworthy was an Overseer mentioned in this Account Book.

If I choose H346.001, however, (Accounts Papers concerning Leusdon & Widecombe School including attendances and payments to pupils, 1901) for further examination, after clicking on 'More Details' I will see a document page as in Figure D-7.

FIGURE D-7: THE WIDECOMBE DIGITAL ARCHIVE DETAILED INFORMATION FOR CATALOGUE ENTRY H346.001

(COPYRIGHT WIDECOMBE HISTORY GROUP)

This shows the information recorded against catalogue number H346.001. A look down the list of names reveals the following entries in Figure D-8:

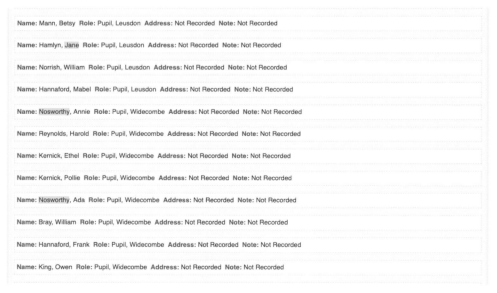

FIGURE D-8: THE WIDECOMBE DIGITAL ARCHIVE DETAIL FROM THE 'DETAILED INFORMATION FOR A CATALOGUE ENTRY' PAGE

(COPYRIGHT WIDECOMBE HISTORY GROUP)

Here we can see the values we searched for highlighted in yellow and we can see it picked up that catalogue entry H346.001 does indeed contain both the words 'nosworthy' and 'jane'. However, the results might not be quite as expected as there is no name Nosworthy, Jane, only a 'Hamlyn, Jane' and a 'Nosworthy, Annie' (and another Ada - and in fact several more in the full list). These results are because the search is looking for 'nosworthy' and 'jane' occurring anywhere in the text, not necessarily together. To search for them together we need to use the *Name Search*.

Note that the Basic Search incorporates an automatic synonym test. For some more tips on using the Basic Search, click on 'Show/Hide Tips' next to the Basic Search heading.

NAME SEARCH

As mentioned in the previous section, the name search enables us to search for a first and last name that are 'together', i.e. as a name rather than as a pair of text strings that occur somewhere in the text.

The approach is very similar to that of the Basic Search described above. You enter a value, a surname, in the 'Search for Last (or Family) Name' box and another value, a first name, in the 'and for First (or Other) Name' box and then click on the 'Search' button.

The site will search the selected collection or collections for the values provided, searching for them *as names* and will return a list of the items that contain the value or values that you have entered.

You can then browse the list that has been returned and select any for more detailed viewing by clicking on the 'More Details' button on the right-hand-side of the row that is of interest.

Name Search: Show/Hide Tips

Search for Last (or Family) Name: nosworthy
and for First (or Other) Name: jane   Search   Clear Form

FIGURE D-9: THE WIDECOMBE DIGITAL ARCHIVE NAME SEARCH BOX

(COPYRIGHT WIDECOMBE HISTORY GROUP)

This time you will get only two results with the choice of 'nosworthy' and 'jane', because there are only two entries that have both of those values in association as a name as shown in Figure D-10.

Search Results:

You can look at details for an individual entry by clicking on the 'More Details' button next to the entry.

Total Number of Items Found: 2 Displaying Page 1 of 1 — Go to Page: 1 | First Page | Previous Page | Next Page | Last Page

Catalogue Number	Type of Item	Brief Description	Date(s) of Item	Images	More
A029.p153	Ledger	Surveyors of the Highways Account Book for the Parish of Widecombe - Division of Dudon (Jordan) - pages 11 to 15 of account year 1844-45	11.4.1844 - 10.4.1845	10	More Details
P002.B28	Headstone	Headstone of Mary Jane Nosworthy. Date: 08.Feb.1905	08.02.1905	3	More Details

Total Number of Items Found: 2 Displaying Page 1 of 1 — Go to Page: 1 | First Page | Previous Page | Next Page | Last Page

FIGURE D-10: THE WIDECOMBE DIGITAL ARCHIVE NAME SEARCH RESULTS BOX

(COPYRIGHT WIDECOMBE HISTORY GROUP)

The name search is clearly more accurate at picking up names and so should always be used if a specific name is being searched for. Note that it is only different to the basic search if you have both a first and a surname. If you just have a surname, then the basic search does just as well.

Note that the Name Search also incorporates an automatic synonym test. For some more tips on using the Name Search, click on 'Show/Hide Tips' next to the Name Search heading.

ADVANCED SEARCH

The final search that you can do is the Advanced Search. This is basically a combination of the basic and name searches with the additional option of searching for a date or date range as well. So, if you are only interested in a particular time period then you can enter it in the Advanced Search boxes. Also, if you don't want the synonym search to be used to extend the range of the search then you can switch it off by using the Advanced Search. This option is hidden by default but can be shown simply by clicking on 'Show/Hide Advanced Search Options' next to the Advanced Search heading.

APPENDIX E FINDING SOMETHING FROM THIS BOOK IN THE ARCHIVE

Once you are familiar with using the Widecombe Digital Archive Website (e.g. by reading through Appendix D and trying out the examples) then it is straightforward to find the items referenced in the present volume.

You can do this using the basic search by entering the catalogue reference number in the first search box. Note, however, that this will only work with items that are in the Widecombe Archive. Images reproduced, for example, from the SW Heritage Trust Devon Archives are not in the Widecombe Archive and so are not accessible this way. You will need to visit SW Heritage Trust in Exeter to view them.

So, just using one example, from Figure 7-23 from Chapter 7, which is the detail from the Overseers' Accounts for 1814/5 concerning the burial suit for Robert French and the costs of burial. This is taken from the page of the Overseers' Accounts under catalogue reference A007.005.p011 as stated in the caption. So, if you enter 'A007.005.p011' in the basic search field we should expect to return that one record. What we actually get is one record with catalogue number A007.005.p001. That is because A007.005.p001, which is catalogue entry 'Widecombe Overseers' Accounts 1810-1824, account year 1814/1815 part 1', consists of eleven images (basically eleven pages of accounts cover the first part of the 1814/1815 accounts).[87] The image in Figure 7-23 is from page 11 of those accounts. If you click on 'More Details' then the catalogue details appear and scrolling down you will come to page 11 which should be highlighted. Click on the image thumbnail to view the image from which the Figure was taken.

_____

[87] The cataloguing process generally divided up large documents into manageable chunks, so the Overseers' Accounts were divided by accounting year and occasionally, as in this case, a year was further sub-divided. This was to prevent an individual catalogue entry becoming too lengthy.

APPENDIX F THE VALUE OF MONEY

It is instructive, although quite difficult, to compare monetary values from the 18th and 19th centuries with those of today.

It would appear from the measuring worth website (well worth a visit):

https://www.measuringworth.com/index.php

that income generally has increased much more than the cost of items, so goods and services are much more affordable today (no doubt as a result of mass-production and the impact of the consumer society), and so if we want to try to gauge the true cost of an item to someone in say 1805 we should use a common measure such as the retail price index (RPI) for all amounts we want to compare. So if we feed in the amount of the Poor Rate collected in 1805 according to the Overseers' Accounts for that year (approx £317-17s), we will find that the equivalent RPI value for 2018 is £25,300, which is quite a substantial sum. The Churchwardens' Church Rate amount of £45 -10s is equivalent to £3,627.

If the relative income levels are used instead of the Retail Price Index, which may be a better measure,[88] then the figure for the Poor Rate is more striking. In this case the average earnings figure for the £317-17s is £301,000.

It is also interesting to note that inflation did not really take off until World War I (1914-1918). In fact, an RPI value of 1.58 in 1805 was 1.336 in 1914 (i.e. RPI had actually fallen over the intervening period), but by 1950 it was 3.742 and by 2017 was 121.869, an astonishing increase.

---

[88] In 1805 the cost of goods would have to be met with the level of earnings prevalent at the time not with today's earnings in relation to today's cost of goods.

APPENDIX G THE BRITISH MONETARY SYSTEM

Prior to decimalisation in the United Kingdom (which occurred on 15th February 1971), the UK had a monetary system that originated in Roman times and had survived more or less untouched.

It had the same pound value as we do today, but the pound was divided into twenty shillings of twelve pence (or pennies) each, making 240 pence in every pound. (This was changed by decimalisation to 100 new pence in every pound, thus one new penny was equivalent to 2.4 old pennies).

A penny could be sub-divided into four quarters, called farthings. Thus, there were 960 farthings in a pound allowing a sub-division of the pound of almost 1000.

So, a typical entry in the Overseers' Accounts of £15 11s 4½d means fifteen pounds, eleven shillings and four and a half pence.

APPENDIX H QUESTIONS FOR FURTHER WORK

This Appendix provides some questions that have not been answered in the text and could be fruitful subjects for further study.

No doubt there are many more questions that could be raised. Widecombe would love to hear from you if you have any comments on this book, any answers to these questions, or any further questions that are of interest.

LYDFORD

The Forest Quarter drops out of the accounts about 1818. Do we know why???

HIGHWAYS

What is 'composition money'?

MEDICAL HELP

What was the true nature of the medical help available in the early 1800s?

RAISING THE CHURCH RATE AND POOR RATE

Did they work from a common list of properties and rateable values?

Was there any connection to the tithe list?

In January 1818 there was a repayment to a Mr Sanders of a loan of £233-19-8d. What were the details of this loan and the reasons for it?

How did the amount of money raised and spent vary over time? Is there any correlation between national and international events and the amount of money raised?

What proportion of the money raised as Poor Rate was spent on Examinations and Removal Orders?

POOR-HOUSE

How was the Church House sub-divided when it was used partly as a poor-house?

How was the poor-house segregated from the schoolrooms?

Did Widecombe get its in-poor to do any work?

What was the relationship between the in-poor and the rest of the community given that the Church House is right at the heart of the village?

CHURCH HOUSE

When was the Church House built and for what purpose?

When was the Sexton's Cottage created?

When and who was the last Sexton?

NEWTON ABBOT UNION

What was the truth about the 1894 scandal and what were the outcomes and recommendations of the local government enquiry?

GENERAL

What light, if any, do the manorial and court rolls shed on the general welfare of the people of Widecombe?

BIBLIOGRAPHY

SIDNEY AND BEATRICE WEBB'S BOOKS

Webb, Sidney and Beatrice, *English Local Government: English Poor Law History: Part I: The Old Poor Law*, Longmans, Green and Co, London, 1927

Webb, Sidney and Beatrice, *English Local Government: English Poor Law History: Part II Volume I: The Last Hundred Years*, Longmans, Green and Co, London, 1929

Webb, Sidney and Beatrice, *English Local Government: English Poor Law History: Part II Volume II: The Last Hundred Years*, Longmans, Green and Co, London, 1929

POOR LAW AND OTHER RELEVANT INTERNET REFERENCES

Good overall site on workhouses and the poor law:
http://www.workhouses.org.uk/

Useful description of poor law in operation and brief mention of how it was raised (not much on this): www.vahs.org.uk/vahs/papers/charlesworth.pdf

Friends of Devon's Archives: http://www.foda.org.uk/main/about.htm

OTHER POOR LAW BOOKS AND DOCUMENTS

Beier, A.L., *The Problem of the Poor in Tudor and Early Stuart England*, Methuen, London, 1983

Church, Rosemary (Editor), *The Compleat Parish Officer*, Wiltshire Family History Society, New Edition 1996 (fascinating re-publication of a handbook for Parish Officers published in 1734).

House of Commons Select Committee, *The Parish and the Union, An Analysis of the Evidence Contained in the Twenty-Two Reports of the Select Committee*, 1837 (really interesting contemporary report after complaints about the Poor Law Amendment Act)

Leonard, E.M., *The Early History of English Poor Relief*, Cambridge University Press, Cambridge, 1900.

Nassau William Senior, Sir Edwin Chadwick, *Poor Law Commissioners' Report of 1834*. Copy of the Report made in 1834 by the Commissioners for Inquiring into the Administration and Practical Operation of the Poor Laws. Presented to both Houses of Parliament by Command of His Majesty (Available online at https://oll.libertyfund.org/titles/senior-poor-law-commissioners-report-of-1834)

North, the Hon. Roger, *A Discourse on the Pernicious Tendency of the Laws for the Maintenance and Settlement of the Poor*, published 1753 (but apparently written about 1670 - see Webb, 1927 page 328)

Report of the Poor Law Commissioners on Local Taxation, London, W. Clowes and Sons, 1844. (Viewable online at https://babel.hathitrust.org/cgi/pt?id=mdp.39015070874873&view=1up&seq=7)

Oxley, Geoffrey W., *Poor Relief in England and Wales 1601-1834*, David & Charles, Newton Abbot, 1974 (excellent bibliography)

Price, Kim, *Medical Negligence in Victorian Britain: The Crisis of Care under the English Poor Law c 1834-1900*, Bloomsbury, 2015 (harrowing tales of neglect and mistreatment of workhouse inmates)

Slack, Paul, *The English Poor Law 1531 - 1782*, MacMillan, London, 1990 (good summary plus list of legislation passed)

BOOKS ABOUT THE TITHE SYSTEM

Evans, Eric J., *The Contentious Tithe*, Routledge & Kegan Paul, London, 1976

Roundell, Earl of Selbourne, *Ancient Facts and Fictions Concerning Churches and Tithes*, Second Edition, MacMillan, London, 1892

EDUCATION

Claxton, Ann, *Report on Early Victorian Schools in the Parish of Widecombe in the Moor, Devon 1833 to 1870*, publication forthcoming, 2016

Horn, Pamela, *The Victorian and Edwardian Schoolchild*, Alan Sutton, Gloucester, 1989

Stanbrook, Mary, *Old Dartmoor Schools Remembered*, Quay Publications, Brixham, 1991.

LOCAL AND DARTMOOR BOOKS AND INTERNET RESOURCES

Brown, Mike, *Buckland Overseers' Accounts 1778-1836*, Dartmoor Press

Brown, Mike, *Buckland-in-the-Moor Churchwardens' Accounts 1632-1691*, Dartmoor Press, 1995

Dymond, Robert, *Things New and Old Concerning the Parish of Widecombe in the Moor and Its Neighbourhood*, The Torquay Directory Company Limited, Torquay, 1876.

Stone, David and Sandover, Richard, *Moor Medieval - Exploring Dartmoor in the Middle Ages*, Moor Medieval Study Group, 2019

Vancouver, Charles, *General View of the Agriculture of the County of Devon*, London,1808. Available from:
https://archive.org/details/generalviewagri01vancgoog/page/n10

Whitten, E.H.T. (Tim), *Bonehill - Evolution of a Dartmoor Hamlet*, Ryelands, 2009

Whitten, E.H.T. (Tim), *The Lords of Widecombe and Farmers of Bonehill*, Widecombe History Group, 2019

Widecombe-in-the-Moor Conservation Area Character Appraisal, Dartmoor National Park Authority January 2011. Available from:
https://www.dartmoor.gov.uk/__data/assets/pdf_file/0005/865409/Widecombe-2011.pdf

Woods, Stephen H., *Widecombe-in-the-Moor - A Pictorial History of the Dartmoor Village*, Devon Books, 1996.

Woods, Stephen H., *Uncle Tom Cobley and All - Widecombe-in-the-Moor - Photographs and Memories of Dartmoor's Most Famous Parish*, Halsgrove, 2000.

INDEX